Elementary
Latin Exercises

Elementary Latin Exercises

An Introduction to North and Hillard's Latin Prose Composition

Rev. A. E. Hillard, D.D.
Late High Master of St. Paul's School

AND

C.G. Botting, M.A.
Late Assistant Master at St. Paul's School

Focus Classical Reprints
Focus Publishing
R. Pullins Company
Newburyport MA

PREFACE

THIS elementary book is planned to lead up to North and Hillard's *Latin Prose Composition*, and is meant to be used from the time when a boy begins Latin. Its arrangement is therefore based on the order in which the authors think Accidence is best learnt, and the new portion of Grammar required is stated at the head of each section by references to the *Revised Public School Primer*, the *Shorter Primer* and *Practical Latin Grammar*. The Grammar is not here printed, as in so many Latin Courses, because the authors think that the pupil should learn the portions from a separate Grammar arranged in the recognized order, and so become familiar with its arrangement.

The order adopted is based on the assumption that we need not begin with anything less than a sentence, even though at first that sentence must consist of one word only. Therefore the Indicative Tenses Active of the 1st Conjugation are learnt first, after which the Declensions with simple Case uses are easily introduced. It need hardly be said that only the essentials of Grammar are included, unusual types and words being simply left on one side, and the Vocabulary being reduced within very manageable limits and almost entirely confined to words used by Caesar. The comparatively late introduction of the Verb *to be* (with which so many books begin) is deliberate, the authors believing that the idea of an Object is simpler to a boy's mind than the idea of a Complement. Other points in the order adopted are made plain by the Table of Contents on pp. ix-xii, and the authors believe that this order will commend itself to schoolmasters. It will be seen that the Syntax covered by this book is practically all that is required for the Simple Sentence. North and Hillard's *Latin Prose* begins the Complex Sentences.

A book which is meant to accompany the learning of the essentials of Latin Accidence, and which therefore assumes a certain course of Grammar (though limited) to be a proper way of beginning the study of Latin, is bound to provoke criticism from those who, in the present day, believe that Latin can be taught better, or at least in a more interesting way, without any formal or orderly course of even the essentials of Grammar. The authors offer no apology for differing from those who hold this theory ; in fact, they would rather carry war into the critics' camp. We are all agreed in the desire to get the pupil through the elementary stages as quickly as we can, and to reduce to a minimum the hard labour of formal Grammar. But the tendency of those who are trying experiments is quite dangerously in the direction of shirking it altogether. With hardly any groundwork the pupil is set to translating " easy pieces " from Latin. By the aid of the master, special vocabularies, and notes

he does learn a translation of these pieces, and in process
of time he does learn to associate certain terminations
with certain Cases or certain parts of the Verb. But he
soon finds that to co-ordinate this knowledge he must,
after all, go through the Grammar. The fact is that this
method of learning entirely by observation in the course
of translation is only applicable in any large degree to
languages which are in the main non-flexional and much
nearer to our own in structure than Latin is. In Latin
it is only applicable to a later stage, when the pupil,
being already familiar with what is regular and ordinary,
is capable of having his attention arrested by anything
irregular in his translation—at that stage and in that
way he can complete his knowledge of the grammatical
structure of the language by the study of points raised
in the course of translation. To attempt to teach the
ordinary forms of Latin in this way is to choose the
longest way to the desired end. It is often claimed
for this method that it is more *interesting* "because
instead of having to learn tenses and declensions the
pupil is introduced at once to a real piece of the language
he is learning." This theory bears no relation to actual
fact. The subject-matter of the pieces of Latin which
the boy at this stage is set to unravel has little or no
interest for him. He despises the anecdotes (especially
when the revision time comes), and would far rather, as a
matter of fact, be set to learn the forms of the Latin
language in a straight and orderly way than have them
filter in piecemeal and in confusion. The method of

teaching that has most interest for a boy is the method
that teaches him most quickly.

But even those who admit the necessity of beginning
with a formal course of the essentials of Grammar may
be inclined to criticise the predominance in this book of
exercises from English into Latin. Would it not be
easier for the pupil to be confined at this early stage to
translation from Latin into English? The authors
believe that this latter is the harder process of the two
at this stage of a boy's knowledge. This is hardly the
place for a psychological statement, and they are content
to appeal to experience. But apart from the hardness or
easiness of each operation, the turning of English into
Latin is more conducive than the reverse process to a
quick and accurate grasp of the forms and the meanings
of Cases and Tenses. And if the question of *interest* is
raised, it is certain that the constructive, creative element
in composition absorbs a boy much more completely than
the analytical element involved in translation.

The authors recognize, nevertheless, that both pro-
cesses should go on together, and they have appended
(pp. 160-190) exercises for translation from Latin corresponding in the vocabulary and constructions required to
each section of the English-Latin exercises. But they have
not assigned to these translation exercises the predominant
position in their course.

The exercises of both kinds are carefully restricted to the
knowledge already acquired at each stage, because only
by so restricting them can we secure the inestimable

advantage of making the pupil *feel his progress*—a feeling
which far outweighs any other kind of interest that
can be imported into the process. It is one of the
advantages of Mathematics that by every chapter the
pupil feels that something new and very definite has
been added to his knowledge. The weariness that many
ordinary pupils feel after a time in acquiring Latin is
largely due to the absence of these milestones in the
process by which they are being taught. It is for this
reason that the authors of this book have imposed re-
strictions upon their exercises, and so limited their vocabulary as to give constant practice in the same set of words.
They believe that in this way the elementary stage of
Latin will be passed most quickly.

NOTE

IN the Grammar references given at the head of each section **R.P.** refers to Kennedy's *Revised Latin Primer*, **S.P.** to the *Shorter Primer*, and **P.G.** to Wilkie and Lydall's *Practical Latin Grammar*.

TABLE OF CONTENTS

English-Latin Exercises with Rules (pages 1-159).

ENGLISH-LATIN EXERCISES

Section 1

Grammar : **Present and Future Indicative Active of** *amo.*
R.P. p. 64 : S.P. p. 42 : P.G. p. 124.

TENSES

When we speak of an action we must speak of it as happening either in the Present time or in the Future or in the Past.

In all languages, therefore, the Verb which expresses an action will have three different sets of forms for these three times. These sets of forms are called Present, Future, and Past TENSES. Thus *I love* or *he loves* is said to be a form of the **PRESENT TENSE,** *I shall love* or *he will love* is said to be a form of the **FUTURE TENSE,** *I loved* or *he loved* is said to be a form of the **PAST TENSE.**

THE PRESENT AND FUTURE TENSES IN LATIN AND ENGLISH

In learning the Present and Future of **amo** notice these things :

(1) In English we say *I love* or *I am loving* for the Present Tense. **Latin has one form only for both of these,** viz. amo. So also we say *I shall love* or *I shall be loving* for the Future Tense. **Latin has one form only for both of these,** viz. amabo.

(2) **In English we always express the Subject of the Verb. In Latin this is not necessary if the Subject is a Personal Pronoun.** Thus **amo** means *I love*, **amamus** means *we love*, **amant** means *they love* without any separate word for the Subject.

The reason for this is obvious if you compare the Latin and English tenses. In English the Verb is *love* for the 1st Person Singular and for the 1st, 2nd, and 3rd Persons Plural. In Latin every one of these has a separate form, and thus **the form of the Verb** makes it clear whether the Subject is *I, we, you,* or *they.*

Exercise 1

1. I work.
2. We love.
3. He hastens.
4. We hasten.
5. You work.

6. They love.
7. I hasten.
8. He works.
9. We work.
10. You hasten.

Exercise 2

1. We shall hasten.
2. I shall work.
3. He will love.
4. You will work.
5. They will hasten.

6. I shall love.
7. We shall work.
8. They are fighting.
9. He will hasten.
10. They will work.

Exercise 3

1. He will fight.
2. They are hastening.
3. I shall fight.
4. She works.
5. We hasten.

6. You will fight.
7. I shall hasten.
8. We are fighting.
9. She hastens.
10. She will work.

SECTION 2

Grammar : **Perfect and Imperfect Indicative Active of** *amo.*   R.P. p. 64 : S.P. p. 42 : P.G. p. 124.

THE PAST TENSES
IN LATIN AND ENGLISH

It has been explained that in English we can say *I love* or *I am loving* for the Present Tense, *I shall love* or *I shall be loving* for the Future Tense, and that Latin has only one form for each of these Tenses.

In the same way we can say *I loved* or *I was loving* for the Past Tense. But here Latin is like English in having *two* forms, viz. **amavi** (which is called in the Grammar the **PERFECT** Tense) and **amabam** (which is called the **IMPERFECT** Tense).

In the following exercises wherever the English has the simple Past (e.g. *I loved, we hastened, they fought*) use the first of these, viz. the Perfect Tense ; whenever the English has the longer form (e.g. *I was loving, we were hastening, they were fighting*) use the second, viz. the Imperfect Tense.[1]

N.B.—The form *I was loving* (like *I am loving* in the Present and *I shall be loving* in the Future) is used to make it clear that we are speaking of an action as continuing or in process. Let the pupil think of the sentence *I was climbing a tree when the branch broke* and ask himself whether it would be as well expressed by *I climbed a tree when the branch broke.*

---

[1] In the Exercises the Imperfect Tense will not be introduced until **Ex. 7.**

Exercise 4

1. He fought.
2. You hastened.
3. She wanders.
4. They work.
5. I fought.

6. You fight.
7. We shall wander.
8. We worked.
9. She will hasten.
10. He fights.

Exercise 5

1. He hastened.
2. He will fight.
3. You fought.
4. We hastened.
5. You worked.

6. She fights.
7. I shall wander.
8. They fought.
9. We shall fight.
10. I worked.

Exercise 6

1. I hastened.
2. We fought.
3. She will fight.
4. They hastened.
5. He worked.

6. You will hasten.
7. She loves.
8. They will fight.
9. They worked.
10. They will love.

Exercise 7

1. He was working.
2. He is wandering.
3. We were fighting.
4. She worked.
5. They were hastening.

6. He wanders.
7. I was fighting.
8. You are wandering.
9. We wander.
10. They were working.

Exercise 8

1. They are wandering.
2. She fought.
3. You will wander.
4. I am fighting.
5. They will wander.

6. She wanders.
7. He was hastening.
8. We love.
9. He will wander.
10. We were hastening.

Exercise 9

1. He will wander.
2. You love.
3. I was hastening.
4. She will love.
5. She hastened.

6 We shall wander.
7. You were hastening.
8. You will wander.
9. You were fighting.
10. They were fighting.

Section 3

Grammar : **Perfect, Pluperfect, Future Perfect Indicative Active of** *amo.* R.P. p. 64 : S.P. p. 42 : P.G. pp. 124–5.

THE PERFECT, PLUPERFECT, AND FUTURE PERFECT TENSES

In Exercises 1–9 we have practised the simple ways of expressing an action in the three times (Present, Future, Past), viz. :

	ENGLISH.	LATIN.
PRESENT.	*I love—I am loving.*	**amo.**
FUTURE.	*I shall love—I shall be loving.*	**amabo.**
PAST.	*I loved—I was loving.*	**amavi—amabam.**

But sometimes we want to make it clear that we are speaking of an action as **completed** at a certain time, and this gives rise in all languages to some different sets of forms which are also called tenses.

In English we say *I have loved, I had loved, I shall have loved.* The Latin forms are :

I have loved	**amavi**	[PERFECT TENSE].
I had loved	**amaveram**	[PLUPERFECT TENSE].
I shall have loved	**amavero** [1]	[FUTURE PERFECT TENSE].

It is most important to notice that the first of these Latin tenses is the same as that which expresses the simple **Past.** In fact the Latin " Perfect Tense " has to do double duty:

e.g. **amavi**=*I loved* or *I have loved.*

pugnaverunt=*they fought* or *they have fought.*

---

[1] For the convenience of practice the Future Perfect will not be introduced until Ex. 13.

Exercise 10

1. I have worked.
2. You will sail.
3. I had fought.
4. He sailed.
5. We have hastened.
6. She sails.
7. She had hastened.
8. They sailed.
9. He has hastened.
10. You have worked.

Exercise 11

1. I had worked.
2. You had fought.
3. We sailed.
4. He has worked.
5. He was sailing.
6. You have hastened.
7. He had fought.
8. I was sailing.
9. They have hastened.
10. They were sailing.

Exercise 12

1. He will sail.
2. We were sailing.
3. We have worked.
4. You sailed.
5. I have hastened.
6. You have worked.
7. We shall sail.
8. You have wandered.
8. We had fought.
10. They are sailing.

Exercise 13

1. We shall have worked.
2. I had wandered.
3. You will have fought.
4. He had sailed.
5. He will have worked.
6. You had wandered.
7. He will have fought.
8. He has wandered.
9. He had wandered.
10. They will have hastened.

Exercise 14

1. We had sailed.
2. We shall have fought.
3. You will have worked.
4. We had wandered.
5. She has sailed.
6. You will have fought.
7. I have wandered.
8. She had sailed.
9. They will have worked.
10. They had sailed.

Exercise 15

1. She has wandered.
2. They will have fought.
3. We have wandered.
4. He has sailed.
5. You will have hastened.
6. You had sailed.
7. They have wandered.
8. He will have hastened.
9. They had wandered.
10. I had sailed.

SECTION 4

Grammar : **Nouns of 1st Declension.**
R.P. p. 17 : S.P. p. 7 : P.G. p. 8.

NOMINATIVE AND ACCUSATIVE CASES— AGREEMENT OF VERB WITH ITS SUBJECT

If we take the simplest English sentence with a Transitive Verb we learn in English Grammar to divide it thus :

	SUBJECT.	VERB.	OBJECT.
e.g.	*The king*	*rules*	*the city.*
	We	*honour*	*him.*

and with regard to these three parts of the sentence we learn these rules :

(1) **The Subject is in the Nominative Case.**

(2) **The Object is in the Objective or Accusative Case.**

(3) **The Verb agrees with its Subject in Number and Person.**

These rules apply to Latin also ;

> e.g. *You love your fatherland.*
> **Amatis patriam.**
>
> *Cotta announced a victory.*
> **Cotta victoriam nuntiavit.**

N.B.—Remember (p. 2) that if the subject is a Personal Pronoun it need not be expressed in Latin, as in the first of the above examples.

Exercise 16

1. They will love their [1] native country.
2. They were attacking the Belgians.
3. The Belgians report the victory.
4. Cotta will attack the Belgians.
5. The Belgians had loved their country.
6. We shall attack Cotta.
7. He had reported the victory.
8. The Belgians loved battles.
9. Cotta has attacked the Belgians.
10. He will attack the forces.

Exercise 17

1. They had reported the victory.
2. Cotta had attacked the Belgians.
3. The Belgians love their country.
4. They are attacking the Belgians.
5. Cotta will report the battle.
6. The Belgians attacked Cotta.
7. You will report the victory.
8. We had reported the victory.
9. The Belgians attacked the forces.
10. Cotta will have reported the victory.

---

[1] In this and the following exercises the Possessive Adjectives *my*, *your*, *their*, etc., need not be expressed in Latin.

Exercise 18

1. We shall have reported the victory.
2. You will attack Cotta.
3. Cotta had attacked the forces.
4. I shall announce the victory.
5. The Belgians will have attacked Cotta.
6. Cotta was attacking the Belgians.
7. You will report the battle.
8. Cotta loved his country.
9. He had attacked the Belgians.
10. Cotta had reported the battle.

SECTION 5

VOCATIVE, GENITIVE, DATIVE
ABLATIVE CASES

A Latin noun has **six Cases,** i.e. six forms of the word to be used according to the part the word takes in the sentence.

We have already seen (p. 10) that

(1) The **Nominative** form is used when the word is the **Subject of the Verb.**

(2) The **Accusative** form is used when the word is the **Object of the Verb.**

In the next set of exercises the other Cases must be practised according to the following rules :

(3) The **Vocative** form is to be used when we address a person directly ;

> e.g.   *Labienus, you will fight.*
> **Labiene, pugnabis.**

(4) The **Genitive** form is to be used to express the **Possessor,** like the English *Possessive Case* ;

> e.g.   *They were attacking* { *the Belgians' forces.*
> { *the forces of the Belgians.*
> **Belgarum copias oppugnabant.**

(5) The **Dative** form is to be used to express what we call
the **Indirect Object.**

This is best understood by thinking of some English sentences ; e.g. *We gave the beggar money.* The Verb in this
sentence appears to govern two objects. But what we gave
was *money*, and this word is the real object of the Verb (to be
expressed by the Accusative Case). The word *beggar* explains
to whom we gave money, and this is called the **Indirect Object**
of the Verb. So in the sentence *Tell the king the news*, the
word *news* is the real Object, the word *king* is the Indirect
Object.

In English we have only one form for the Objective Case,
and therefore we most often use a Preposition to express the
Indirect Object ; e.g. We gave money *to the beggar*, Tell the
news *to the king.*

But in Latin there is a separate case, viz. the Dative, to
express the Indirect Object ;

> e.g.   *They report a victory to the Belgians.*
> **Victoriam Belgis nuntiant.**

(6) The **Ablative** form is to be used to express the **instrument** by which or with which we do something. In English
we can only express this by Prepositions ;

> e.g.   *They wounded the Belgians with arrows.*
> **Belgas sagittis vulneraverunt.**

Exercise 19

1. We love our native country.
2. They are attacking the forces of the Belgians.
3. We reported the victory.
4. Cotta will wound the Belgians.
5. The Belgians love their country.
6. They wounded the Belgians with their arrows.
7. We had reported the victory of Cotta.
8. Cotta attacked the forces of the Belgians.
9. The Belgians reported the victory.
10. The Belgians had attacked the forces of Cotta.

Exercise 20

1. They reported the victory of the Belgians.
2. He assailed the Belgians with arrows.
3. Cotta will save his country by his wisdom.
4. They will wound the Belgians with arrows.
5. They have attacked the forces of Cotta.
6. We shall report the battle to the Belgians.
7. They had attacked the forces of the Belgians with arrows.
8. He had reported the battle to the Belgians.
9. We attacked the forces of the Belgians.
10. He reported the victories of Cotta.

Exercise 21

1. We reported the victory to the Belgians.
2. They attacked the forces of the Belgians with arrows.
3. They will report the victory to Cotta.
4. He will announce the victory of the Belgians.
5. Cotta has saved his country by his wisdom.
6. They will attack the forces of the Belgians.
7. They will save their country by their wisdom.
8. They will announce the victory to the Belgians.
9. The Belgians saved their country by wisdom.
10. We were attacking the forces of the Belgians.

Section 6

Grammar : **Nouns of 2nd Declension in -us.**
R.P. p. 18 : S.P. p. 8 : P.G. p. 14.

Exercise 22

1. The barbarians loved their native country.
2. We overcame the Romans.
3. The Romans did not like the Belgians.
4. They wounded Labienus with an arrow.
5. They announced the victory of the Romans.
6. They wounded the barbarians' horses with arrows.
7. The Romans will defeat the barbarians.
8. Labienus attacked the barbarians.
9. Cotta will announce a victory to the Romans.
10. The barbarians have wounded Labienus with an arrow.

Exercise 23

1. The Romans will have defeated the barbarians.
2. Our men attacked the forces of the Belgians.
3. Our men overcame the barbarians.
4. Labienus saved his country.
5. Our men were wounding the barbarians with arrows.
6. The Romans and Belgians will fight.
7. He will defeat the Romans.
8. Labienus, you do not love your country.
9. We had saved our country by our wisdom.
10. The Belgians will attack the Romans.

Exercise 24

1. Our men had wounded the Belgians with arrows.

2. Labienus, you will not defeat the Belgians.

3. Our men are wounding the barbarians' horses.

4. Our men will overcome the Belgians.

5. The barbarians assailed our men with arrows.

6. Our men will attack the forces of the barbarians.

7. The Romans had assailed the Belgians with arrows.

8. You had announced the victory of our men.

9. We attacked the forces of the barbarians.

10. The barbarians attacked the forces of the Belgians.

Section 7

Grammar : **Nouns of 2nd Declension in -um.**
R.P. p. 18 : S.P. p. 8 : P.G. p. 20.

Exercise 25

1. The barbarians were preparing war.
2. Our men overcame the barbarians.
3. They assailed the forces of the barbarians with weapons.
4. They saved the town by their plan
5. The weapons were wounding the Romans' horses.
6. The stratagem of the Romans saved the towns.
7. Labienus, you avoided the dangers of the war.
8. The barbarians assailed the towns.
9. Cotta saved the towns by a stratagem.
10. Labienus, you will not avoid the danger.

Exercise 26

1. The Belgians attacked Cotta's camp.
2. The weapons of our men are wounding the Belgians' horses.
3. The Romans will overcome the Belgians.
4. The barbarians defeated our men by a stratagem.
5. Our men are assailing the camp of the barbarians.
6. The forces of the Romans will save the town.
7. You will not overcome the Belgians.
8. Our men assailed the Belgians with their weapons.
9. We shall not overcome the Romans by stratagem.
10. The Romans loved wars and battles.

Exercise 27

1. Our men had assailed the towns of the barbarians.
2. Our men will attack the camp of the Belgians.
3. We shall attack the camp of the Romans.
4. Labienus had avoided the dangers of war.
5. The Belgians are assailing the camp with arrows.
6. The barbarians assailed the towns of the Romans.
7. We announced to the Romans the victories of the barbarians.
8. The victory of our men saved the camp.
9. Romans, you will prepare war.
10. By your wisdom you avoided the dangers of war.

Section 8

Grammar : **Nouns of 2nd Declension in -er.**
R.P. p. 18 : S.P. p. 8 : P.G. p. 18.

Exercise 28

1. The boys loved wars and battles.
2. We laid waste the fields of the barbarians.
3. Our men will lay waste the fields of the Belgians.
4. Boys love horses.
5. The barbarians built towns.
6. The boys saved the town by their device.
7. They wounded the boy's horse with an arrow.
8. The boys were hastening.
9. He wounded the boy with an arrow.
10. I shall attack the camp of the barbarians.

Exercise 29

1. The boys announced the victory of the Belgians.
2. We shall lay waste the field of the Belgians.
3. Boys do not love wisdom.
4. You did not lay waste the fields of the Gauls.
5. The boys avoided the dangers of the war.
6. We are preparing war, Romans.
7. The Gauls wounded the boy's horse with a weapon.
8. The boys will save the town by their device.
9. The weapons of the Gauls were wounding the boys.
10. You have laid waste the fields of the Romans.

Exercise 30

1. He had laid waste the fields of the Gauls.
2. The boys will avoid the danger.
3. The wisdom of the boys saved the town.
4. We attacked the camp of the Gauls.
5. The Gauls saved their camp by a stratagem.
6. Our men will lay waste the fields of the barbarians.
7. The Romans overcame the Gauls by a stratagem.
8. We assailed the Gauls with weapons
9. The Gauls had built towns.
10. Boys love danger.

Section 9

Grammar : **Present, Future, Imperfect, and Perfect Indicative Active of** *moneo.* R.P. p. 66 : S.P. p. 44 : P.G. p. 128.

Adjectives in -*us*. R.P. p. 37 : S.P. p. 20 : P.G. p. 64.

THE AGREEMENT OF ADJECTIVES WITH NOUNS

English Adjectives have no terminations to mark Gender or Number or Case. Hence we do not need to make them " agree " with the Noun to which they belong. In Latin the Adjective is declined as well as the Noun.

An Adjective agrees with its Noun in Gender, Number, and Case.

	e.g.	*A good field*	*A small arrow*	*A large town*
NOM. SING.		bonus ager	parva sagitta	magnum oppidum
GEN. SING.		boni agri	parvae sagittae	magni oppidi
ACC. PLU.		bonos agros	parvas sagittas	magna oppida

N.B.—An Adjective can sometimes be used without a Noun. This is especially the case with the Masculine, when the word *man* or *men* is understood.

> e.g.   *A good man loves a good man.*
> **Bonus bonum amat.**
>
> *Good men* (or *the good*) *love good men.*
> **Boni bonos amant.**

Exercise 31

1. Our men feared the great forces of the Gauls.
2. The Romans had small weapons.
3. The Gauls built small towns.
4. We overcame the great forces of the barbarians.
5. The Gauls had good horses.
6. By their great wisdom they avoided the dangers of war.
7. The arrows frightened the little boys.
8. We were attacking the great forces of the Belgians.
9. They reported a great victory
10. The barbarians will not fear our men.

Exercise 32

1. We shall not have large forces.
2. You feared the small forces of the barbarians.
3. Good men do not fear danger.
4. The Belgians had small arrows.
5. The barbarians feared the small forces of the Romans.
6. Small dangers will not frighten the Gauls.
7. You have great wisdom.
8. He fears the great dangers of war.
9. The Belgians had good horses.
10. Small forces of Romans attacked the Gauls' camp.

Exercise 33

1. Our men's great victory saved the town.
2. Cotta fears the large forces of the Belgians.
3. The barbarians had good fields.
4. He wounded the little boy with a large arrow.
5. Great dangers do not frighten good men.
6. You will not fear the great forces of the Gauls.
7. The barbarians have small horses.
8. Our men were frightening the Gauls with their large weapons.
9. They were wounding our men with small arrows.
10. We shall attack the great forces of the barbarians.

SECTION 10

Grammar : **Future Perfect and Pluperfect Indicative Active of** *moneo.* R.P. p. 66 : S.P. p. 44 : P.G. p. 129.
Adjectives in -er (2nd and 1st Declension forms).
R.P. p. 38 : S.P. p. 21 : P.G. p. 70.

Exercise 34

1. The wretched boys were working.
2. The Gauls have beautiful towns.
3. We had frightened the barbarians with our darts.
4. The barbarians had feared the dangers of war.
5. The Belgians had small shields.
6. You frightened the wretched prisoners.
7. He had frightened the wretched barbarians.
8. Unhappy men do not fear the dangers of war.
9. You have not frightened our men.
10. We shall not have feared the great forces of the Gauls.

Exercise 35

1. The Gauls had frightened the wretched prisoners.

2. Our men laid waste the beautiful towns of the Belgians.

3. By his plan he saved the wretched prisoners.

4. You will frighten the little boys.

5. The Gauls' weapons were wounding the wretched prisoners.

6. The barbarians have large shields.

7. Wars and dangers do not frighten good men.

8. We had frightened the great forces of the Gauls.

9. The wretched men did not avoid the barbarians' arrows.

10. By your plan you will save our men.

Exercise 36

1. The wretched prisoners had not weapons.

2. The arrows of the Gauls will not have frightened our men.

3. By his great wisdom he will overcome a great danger.

4. The Gauls had good fields and beautiful towns.

5. The wretched prisoners have not shields.

6. He had frightened the wretched captive.

7. He announced to the unhappy man the victory of the Romans.

8. The wretched prisoner had not a horse.

9. The great victory of the Gauls had frightened our men.

10. We shall lay waste the Gauls' beautiful towns.

SECTION 11

Grammar : **Present, Future, Imperfect, and Perfect Indicative Active of** *rego.* R.P. p. 68 : S.P. p. 46 :
P.G. p. 132.

Exercise 37

1. We shall lead large forces of the Romans against the
barbarians.
2. He neglected the good advice of Cotta.
3. The barbarians had not many arrows.
4. Cotta led large forces of Romans against the Belgians.
5. We rule the land of the barbarians.
6. You will rule your native country.
7. They wounded many Belgians with their arrows.
8. You will not neglect good advice.
9. We shall not fear the barbarians' arms.
10. We shall lead the Roman forces into the camp.

Exercise 38

1. The Belgians will lead their forces into the town.
2. Cotta led his forces into camp.
3. Many men do not fear danger.
4. We led the captives into the town.
5. He will lead his forces against the barbarians.
6. He rules his country with great wisdom.
7. You led the Roman forces against the Belgians.
8. The barbarians are leading their forces into the camp.
9. By his wisdom he avoided the many dangers of war.
10. The boys led the horses into the field.

Exercise 39

1. They led the Roman captives into the barbarians' camp.
2. By his many victories he has saved his country.
3. We rule many lands by arms.
4. The barbarians' arms frightened the boys.
5. He is leading our men into the fields.
6. They will lead the Roman captives into the camp.
7. He did not neglect the advice of the Romans.
8. We do not fear the stratagems of the Belgians.
9. The Gauls have built many towns.
10. We shall rule the wretched barbarians.

SECTION 12

Grammar : **Future Perfect and Pluperfect Indicative Active
of *rego*.** R.P. p. 68 : S.P. p. 46 : P.G. p. 133
Nouns (Consonant stems) of 3rd Declension.[1]
R.P. pp. 22–24 : S.P. pp. 12–14 : P.G. pp. 24–44.

Exercise 40

1. The general has led his forces into the town.

2. The soldiers are announcing the victory to the general.

3. He had led the wretched captives into the camp.

4. You will have ruled many towns, you will have saved
your country.

5. The Gauls had led their forces into camp.

6. The Roman soldiers were wounding the Gauls with their
darts.

7. He had neglected the advice of the guide.

8. The Roman soldiers had not good guides.

9. The cavalry attacked the camp with darts and arrows.

10. They had announced to the general the victory of the
cavalry.

---

[1] A summary of the rules for *Gender* will be found on pp. 156–158.
But for the present the Gender of every Noun required in the Exercises
is given in the Vocabularies.

Exercise 41

1. You will have led your soldiers into great danger.

2. They announced to the general the soldiers' victory.

3. We did not neglect the general's advice.

4. They will lead the Roman cavalry against the barbarians.

5. I had led my forces into the Roman camp.

6. The soldier's device saved the town.

7. The victory of the Roman cavalry terrified the Belgians.

8. The barbarians had not good leaders.

9. Good soldiers love a good general.

10. He had led the cavalry against the Belgians.

Exercise 42

1. The little boys frightened the soldiers' horses.

2. Our men announced the victory to their leaders.

3. The Belgians' weapons were wounding the Roman soldiers.

4. We had led our men into the fields.

5. He announced the general's plan to the Belgians.

6. You will not have neglected the general's advice.

7. They reported the victory to the Roman general.

8. The Roman cavalry had large horses.

9. You had led your soldiers into the fields of the barbarians.

10. Cotta will lead the Roman cavalry into the town.

Section 13

Grammar : **Present, Future, Imperfect, and Perfect Indicative Active of** *audio.* R.P. p. 70 : S.P. p. 48 : P.G. p. 136.

Nouns (I stems) of 3rd Declension.

R.P. pp. 25–27 : S.P. pp. 15, 16 : P.G. pp. 47–52.

Exercise 43

1. The soldiers hear the general's shout.
2. The Belgians fortified their towns with ramparts.
3. We shall hear the cries of the soldiers.
4. We shall attack the enemy's camp.
5. They led large forces of cavalry against the enemy.
6. The general heard the loud cries of the enemy.
7. Labienus fortified his camp with a large rampart.
8. The Belgians are fortifying their towns.
9. Cotta had attacked large forces of the enemy.
10. The shouts of the cavalry terrified the Belgians.

Exercise 44

1. The leaders of the enemy led their forces into camp.
2. We shall fortify the camp with a large rampart.
3. The cavalry hear the loud shouts of the barbarians.
4. Cotta had led his forces against the enemy.
5. The wretched soldiers heard the shouts of the enemy.
6. You will hear the shouts of the Roman citizens.
7. They announced to the Belgians the victory of the Roman general.
8. We shall not fear the small forces of the enemy.
9. The enemy had large forces of cavalry.
10. The Roman soldiers will fortify the town with ramparts.

Exercise 45

1. The weapons of the enemy were wounding our men.

2. They will lead large forces of the enemy against the town.

3. We shall hear the shouts of the wretched captives.

4. The leaders of the cavalry had avoided danger.

5. We are fortifying the town with a large rampart.

6. Cotta led large forces of cavalry against the enemy.

7. The Belgians were fortifying their camp and their towns.

8. Labienus heard the loud shouts of the Gauls.

9. We shall not fear the arms of the enemy.

10. The barbarians are fortifying their towns with ramparts.

Section 14

Grammar : **Future Perfect and Pluperfect Indicative Active of** *audio.* R.P. p. 70 : S.P. p. 48 : P.G. p. 137.
Adjectives of 3rd Declension.
R.P. pp. 39, 40 : S.P. pp. 22, 23 : P.G. pp. 72–74.

Exercise 46

1. The Gauls had fortified their camp with a huge rampart.
2. He has avoided all the dangers of war.
3. We had heard the shouts of the wretched citizens.
4. The cavalry laid waste all the fields of the Gauls.
5. The barbarians had huge shields.
6. All the towns of the Belgians had ramparts.
7. Cotta had fortified the camp with a small rampart.
8. Huge forces of the enemy attacked our men.
9. He avoided all the enemy's arrows.
10. The barbarians have fortified all their towns.

Exercise 47

1. Labienus led all the cavalry into camp.
2. We have fortified the city with a huge rampart.
3. He reported to the general all the enemy's plans.
4. Our men will attack the huge forces of cavalry.
5. All the barbarians were preparing war.
6. The Romans had large cities, the Gauls small towns.
7. They had fortified all their cities with ramparts.
8. By your wisdom you had avoided all the dangers of war.
9. Labienus will have heard the loud shouts of the enemy.
10. The cavalry have neglected the general's advice.

Exercise 48

1. The Belgians had fortified the small city with a large rampart.

2. All heard the cries of the soldiers.

3. Huge weapons will not terrify the Roman forces.

4. The boys saved the city by their shouts.

5. Huge forces of the Belgians are attacking the Roman camp.

6. All the barbarians neglected the advice of their leaders.

7. We overcame all the forces of the enemy.

8. The Romans had beautiful cities.

9. Labienus will fortify his camp with a small rampart.

10. You have heard the cries of the wretched citizens.

PASSIVE VOICE

When we use a Transitive Verb in the Active Voice the Subject is the doer of the action.

When we use it in the Passive Voice the Subject is the person or thing acted upon ;

e.g.   Active : *The king built this house.*

       Passive : *This house was built by the king.*

Thus the Direct Object in the Active form of the sentence becomes the Subject in the Passive form. When the Verb is Transitive the same sense can always be expressed in either form.[1]

e.g.   *They are attacking the city.*
       Urbem oppugnant.

       The city is being attacked.
       Urbs oppugnatur.

When the Verb is Passive the agent or doer of the action is expressed by using the Preposition *a* or *ab* with the Ablative Case.

e.g.   *The Gauls are attacking the Romans*
       Galli Romanos oppugnant.

       The Romans are being attacked by the Gauls.
       Romani a Gallis oppugnantur.

N.B.—It is important to distinguish the *agent* and the *instrument*. The former is a *living being*. The rule for expressing instrument has already been given on p. 14.

---

[1] When the Verb is Intransitive there cannot be a Passive. Thus you cannot express *I tremble, the river flows,* or *they run* in a Passive shape. In Latin, however, there is a certain use of an Intransitive Verb in the Passive (3rd Person) which will be explained later on.

Before doing the exercises notice also the following points :—

(1) The *Indirect* Object of the Active Verb (see p. 14) will remain unchanged in the Passive form of the sentence ;

e.g.   *The soldier will announce the victory to the general.*
Miles victoriam imperatori nuntiabit.

   The victory will be announced to the general by the soldier.
Victoria a milite imperatori nuntiabitur.

(2) It will be learnt from the Grammar that the **Perfect, Pluperfect and Future Perfect** Tenses of the Passive Voice are made up of the Past Participle of the Verb and forms of the Verb *sum*, I am. **The Participle in these forms must be made to agree with the Subject just like an Adjective** (see p. 22) ;

e.g.   *We have been wounded.*
Vulnerati sumus.

   The city was saved.
Urbs servata est.

SECTION 15

Grammar : **Present, Future, Perfect, and Imperfect Indicative Passive of** *amo.* R.P. p. 72 : S.P. p. 50 : P.G. p. 126.

Exercise 49

1. The Gauls were wounded by our men's darts.
2. The barbarians were defeated by our men.
3. Many towns of the Gauls were laid waste.
4. The Roman soldiers were being wounded by the barbarians' arrows.
5. The horses will be wounded by the darts.
6. Many burdens were being carried by the captives.
7. The cities will be saved by the general's plan.
8. The cavalry were attacked by the barbarians.
9. You will be defeated by Labienus.
10. The victory is being announced to the Roman general.

Exercise 50

1. The fields of the Gauls will not be laid waste by our men.
2. A few barbarians were wounded by arrows.
3. The Belgians had fortified all their towns with ramparts.
4. Huge burdens were being carried by our men.
5. All the fields of the Gauls are being laid waste.
6. Few heard the loud shouts of the barbarians.
7. The camp of the enemy was attacked by our men.
8. All the dangers of war were avoided by the leader.
9. The huge forces of cavalry were attacked by the enemy.
10. We all fear the enemy's cavalry.

Exercise 51

1. War is being prepared by the enemies of the city.
2. All the forces of the barbarians will be attacked.
3. The wretched citizens had few leaders.
4. Many towns are being built by the barbarians.
5. A few citizens heard the shouts of the enemy.
6. The huge burdens will be carried by the captives.
7. We are being defeated by small forces of the Belgians.
8. All the soldiers avoided the enemy's darts.
9. He is loved by all the citizens
10. We shall be defeated by the cavalry of the Gauls.

Section 16

Grammar : **Future Perfect and Pluperfect Indicative Passive of** *amo.* R.P. p. 72 : S.P. p. 50 : P.G. p. 127

Exercise 52

1. The city will have been saved by the citizens.
2. All the fields of the Gauls had been laid waste.
3. The victory had been reported by a boy.
4. A few towns will be laid waste by the soldiers.
5. The leaders of the enemy heard the shouts of the infantry.
6. The horses had been wounded with arrows.
7. The infantry are avoiding all dangers.
8. The camp is being attacked by the Belgians.
9. Few victories have been announced to the Romans.
10. The dangers of war will be avoided by our men.

Exercise 53

1. The general had been wounded by the enemy's darts.
2. The Roman cavalry have laid waste all the fields.
3. The town had been built by the Gauls.
4. The Roman infantry were defeated by the Belgians.
5. The barbarians are frightening the citizens with their shouts.
6. He had fortified a few cities with ramparts.
7. You were wounded by an arrow.
8. Huge burdens had been carried by the captives.
9. Cotta led his infantry against the barbarians.
10. The cavalry of the enemy will have been defeated.

Exercise 54

1. The camp has been attacked by large forces of cavalry.

2. The infantry neglected the advice of Labienus.

3. Our men will have been defeated by the barbarians.

4. The town is being laid waste by the Belgians.

5. Cotta is fortifying his camp with a huge rampart.

6. All the burdens were carried by the soldiers.

7. The city has been saved by the infantry.

8. All heard the loud cries of the barbarians.

9. He announced the victory to the leader of the Roman forces.

10. A few citizens were wounded with darts.

SECTION 17

Grammar : **Present, Future, Imperfect, and Perfect Indicative Passive of** *moneo.* R.P. p. 74 : S.P. p. 52 : P.G. p. 130.

Exercise 55

1. The Romans are not frightened by the shouts of the enemy.

2. A good general is not feared by his soldiers.

3. The cavalry were not frightened by the shouts of the barbarians.

4. Small dangers are not feared by our men.

5. We were not frightened by the enemy's darts.

6. We are feared by all the barbarians.

7. The leader of the enemy was feared by our men.

8. The town was built by the Gauls.

9. You will not be frightened by the small forces of the enemy.

10. The city is held by Cotta.

Exercise 56

1. The Roman people were feared by the Gauls.

2. A part of the cavalry was attacking the enemy's camp.

3. All the cities are held by the barbarians.

4. All the Belgians feared the Roman people.

5. We defeated a part of the infantry.

6. Huge forces of the enemy had seized the city.

7. We have already defeated a part of the Roman forces.

8. All cities fear the Romans.

9. The victory was announced to the Roman people.

10. The Belgians defeated a great part of our men.

Exercise 57

1. The forces of Labienus seized a large city.

2. The cavalry will not be frightened by the shouts of the Gauls.

3. The dangers of war are not feared by the Roman people.

4. Roman soldiers are not frightened by barbarians.

5. The cities are not held by the enemy.

6. The Roman people ruled the Gauls.

7. The Gauls had already fortified the town with a rampart.

8. The general had already led a great part of his forces into camp.

9. A great part of the land had been seized by the enemy.

10. You will all hear the cries of the soldiers.

Section 18

Grammar : **Future Perfect and Pluperfect Indicative Passive**
of *moneo.* R.P. p. 74 : S.P. p. 52 : P.G. p. 131.
Some Exceptional Nouns of 2nd and 3rd Declensions.
R.P. pp. 19, 26 : S.P. pp. 9, 16 : P.G. pp. 16, 42, 54.

Exercise 58

1. You had already been warned by the general.

2. They had been terrified by the Roman people.

3. We had been warned by the guides.

4. The leader of the enemy will have been already warned.

5. You will be feared by all the barbarians.

6. They will have been terrified by the shouts of the enemy.

7. The Gauls have now been warned by the general.

8. The wretched citizens had been terrified by the cries of
the enemy.

9. The boy had been warned by his father.

10. We shall not neglect the advice of a good general.

Exercise 59

1. You were not warned by your father.
2. The city was saved by the gods.
3. The father led his sons into the city.
4. The barbarians were preparing war by land and sea.
5. The sons had heard the advice of their fathers.
6. The gods have fortified the land with the sea.
7. The wretched citizens were warned by the general.
8. The boys were frightened by the Belgians' arrows.
9. The citizens will be warned by the general.
10. A good father is not feared by his son.

Exercise 60

1. The horses were carrying huge burdens.
2. The citizens have already fortified their city with a rampart.
3. The father was saved by his son's device.
4. We rule the barbarians by land and sea.
5. Good citizens fear the gods.
6. My son, you will not be wounded by your father's arrow.
7. Our men are feared by land and sea.
8. The city has been seized by our men.
9. A part of the cavalry will attack the camp.
10. Part of the city was saved by the general's stratagem.

Section 19

Grammar : **Present, Future, Imperfect, and Perfect Indicative Passive of *rego*.** R.P. p. 76 : S.P. p. 54 ; P.G. p. 134.

Nouns in -*us* of 4th Declension. R.P. p. 30 : S.P. p. 17 : P.G. p. 56.

Exercise 61

1. All armies are led by generals.
2. The Gauls were frightened by our men's fierce attack.
3. The land was ruled by the Romans.
4. We shall be led into many cities.
5. We shall not be ruled by the Roman people.
6. Roman soldiers are being led against their country.
7. They will not be guided by the advice of their fathers.
8. We were terrified by the enemy's fierce attack.
9. Part of the Roman army was attacked by the Gauls.
10. The general's advice was neglected by the soldiers.

Exercise 62

1. We overcame the huge forces of the enemy by a fierce charge.

2. A part of the army was attacking the Belgians' camp.

3. The city was neglected by the army.

4. The infantry are being led against the rampart.

5. The general is leading the army into the town.

6. The father's advice was often neglected by his sons.

7. We withstood the fierce charge of the cavalry.

8. The country is ruled by good leaders.

9. The general's advice will not be neglected by the Roman citizens.

10. The enemy will not withstand the onset of the Roman soldiers.

Exercise 63

1. Many armies were led against the Gauls by the Romans.

2. They announced the victory to the Roman army.

3. War is being prepared by every city.

4. The Gauls' onset was withstood by the whole army.

5. Barbarians often attacked Roman armies.

6. The army will be led into the fields of the Gauls.

7. The barbarians heard the loud cries of the Roman army.

8. The Gauls often fortified their towns with ramparts.

9. Large forces of infantry are being led against the Belgians.

10. You will not be neglected by your father.

Section 20

Grammar : **Future Perfect and Pluperfect Indicative Passive of** *rego.* R.P. p. 76 : S.P. p. 54 : P.G. p. 135.
Nouns in -*u* of 4th Declension. R.P. p. 30 : S.P. p. 17 : P.G. p. 58.

Exercise 64

1. The cavalry had been drawn up on the right wing.
2. The army will be led back into camp.
3. You will not have been neglected by the general.
4. Part of the army has been drawn up by Labienus.
5. The generals are drawing up their forces.
6. The left wing is held by the Roman infantry.
7. A part of the forces has already been led back into the camp.
8. He drew up the Roman cavalry on the right wing.
9. Part of the army has been drawn up opposite to the city.
10. They are announcing the victory to the army.

Exercise 65

1. The Roman soldiers had been drawn up opposite to the rampart.

2. The cavalry will be led back into the Roman camp.

3. The left wing of the army is held by the infantry.

4. A great part of the Roman army was defeated by the enemy.

5. The city had been ruled by the Romans.

6. The advice of the general will not have been neglected.

7. Romans will not be ruled by barbarians.

8. The city is being attacked by the whole army.

9. We shall be guided by the advice of our leaders.

10. Labienus had drawn up the cavalry on the right wing.

Exercise 66

1. The Roman people was feared by all the barbarians.

2. Part of the town had been seized by the army.

3. He is leading back his forces into camp.

4. The Roman army is being led against the forces of the Belgians.

5. The father's advice has not been neglected by his son.

6. Part of the army heard the cries of the citizens.

7. On the right wing our men were being wounded by arrows.

8. The soldiers were withstanding the fierce onsets of the enemy.

9. By a fierce charge we defeated the barbarians.

10. Soldiers, you will be led back into the camp.

Section 21

Grammar : **Present, Future, Imperfect, and Perfect Indicative Passive of** *audio.* R.P. p. 78 : S.P. p. 56 : P.G. p. 138.

Exercise 67

1. The Roman army was hindered by the wood.

2. The cries of the citizens were heard by the general.

3. A great part of the town is being fortified by the citizens.

4. We shall not be prevented by the Roman soldiers.

5. The city was being fortified with a rampart and towers.

6. The voice of the king will be heard by all the soldiers.

7. The citizens are fortifying their town with a huge rampart.

8. The victory of the cavalry will be announced to the king.

9. You will not be heard by the enemy's leaders.

10. All the towns of the Gauls are being fortified.

Exercise 68

1. We shall be hindered by the woods.

2. The Gauls had built many towers.

3. They were being prevented by the general of the Roman army.

4. The king will draw up the infantry on the left wing.

5. A great part of the city will be fortified by a rampart.

6. All the forces of the enemy were drawn up opposite to the tower.

7. The soldiers were being hindered by their burdens.

8. The enemy were withstanding the fierce attack of our men.

9. Huge forces of Gauls had seized a small wood.

10. The loud cries of the barbarians were heard by the Romans.

Exercise 69

1. On the right wing the Belgians withstood our men's attack.

2. The voice of Labienus was heard by his soldiers.

3. The king has led back his cavalry into camp.

4. The land had many woods.

5. The Roman cavalry were drawn up opposite to the enemy's infantry.

6. The shouts of the barbarians will be heard by the whole army.

7. A great part of the city was saved by the Roman general.

8. All the towns will be laid waste by the king's forces.

9. The voice of the wretched is heard by the gods.

10. The cries of the captives are heard by the king.

SECTION 22

Grammar : **Pluperfect and Future Perfect Indicative Passive
of** *audio.* R.P. p. 78 : S.P. p. 56 : P.G. p. 139.
Nouns of 5th Declension. R.P. p. 31 : S.P. p. 18 :
P.G. p. 60.

The word " thing," if qualified by an Adjective or Ad-
jectival Pronoun, is usually expressed by the neuter of that
Adjective or Pronoun, when it is in the Nominative or
Accusative Case ; in other Cases it is expressed by the word
res with the Adjective or Pronoun in agreement ;

> e.g.   *Many things have been prepared.*
> **Multa parata sunt.**
> *I am frightened by many things.*
> **Multis rebus terreor.**

Exercise 70

1. The loud cries of the enemy had already been heard by
our men.

2. Huge forces of barbarians attacked the line of the
Romans.

3. A great part of the city had been fortified with ramparts.

4. Roman soldiers will not be hindered by barbarians.

5. The leader of the army has drawn up his line.

6. Great men are not frightened by small things.

7. Many things hindered our men.

8. The voice of the king has been heard by all the citizens.

9. Caesar had drawn up his line of battle.

10. All the towns of the Gauls were fortified by walls.

Exercise 71

1. The cries of the captives were heard by Caesar.

2. Our men attacked the line of the enemy with darts and arrows.

3. A great part of the city has already been fortified.

4. The line of the enemy was drawn up opposite the Roman camp.

5. The city had been fortified with a large rampart.

6. Already the voices of the soldiers had been heard.

7. The line of the Belgians had been drawn up by their king.

8. The cry of the citizens will have been heard by the whole army.

9. The king had neglected the advice of the citizens.

10. Huge burdens were carried by the king's soldiers.

Exercise 72

1. Everything had been heard by the leader.

2. We were hindered by many things

3. The shouts of the Roman army had not been heard by the barbarians.

4. The king's forces attacked the line of our men.

5. The camp has been fortified with a large rampart.

6. The cavalry was led back into camp by the king.

7. The city has been fortified with a large tower.

8. All things frighten boys and barbarians.

9. Caesar led back a great part of his forces into the wood.

10. The attack of our men was withstood by the enemy's line.

SECTION 23

Grammar : **Indicative of sum.** R.P. p. 62 : S.P. p. 40 :
P.G. pp. 152–3.

THE VERB *SUM*

In a sentence like *The world is* the word *is* means *exists*, and
it makes sense without anything added. But this is not the
commonest use of the Verb *to be*.

In sentences like *He is wise* or *He was king of Britain* the
words *is, was* make no sense without the Adjective or Noun
that follows them.

This Adjective or Noun that, so to speak, completes the
sense of any form of the Verb *to be* or the corresponding Latin
Verb *esse* is called its **Complement** and **must always be in the
same case as the Subject**; furthermore, if it is an **Adjective,
it must agree with the Subject in Number and Gender ;**

e.g. *Romulus was king of the Romans.*
   Romulus rex Romanorum fuit.
   The boys will be happy.
   Pueri felices erunt.

Exercise 73

1. There was a large number of captives in the camp.
2. We shall not be successful.
3. Cotta was the leader of the Roman forces.
4. The walls of the enemy were small.
5. There are many captives in the city.
6. Great was the wisdom of the Roman generals.
7. I am a Roman citizen.
8. The cities of Gaul were not beautiful.
9. The shouts of the barbarians never frightened our men.
10. The Romans were successful in every battle.

Exercise 74

1. The general was fortunate, (but) not daring.
2. He had been the general of a Roman army.
3. You will never be Roman citizens.
4. The plan of the general was daring.
5. The Gauls had never feared an enemy.
6. The boy's father was a soldier.
7. The infantry had never attacked a city.
8. The gods never neglect good men.
9. There were large forces of cavalry in the woods.
10. A small number of citizens withstood the enemy's attack.

Exercise 75

1. The voice of the wretched will always be heard by the gods.
2. The fierce attacks of the enemy will never terrify our men.
3. A large number of the soldiers had been led back into camp.
4. Great plans are often hindered by small things.
5. The weapons of the enemy wounded a large number of our men.
6. Great dangers are never feared by bold men.
7. The cavalry had been drawn up in the wood.
8. Boys are often warned by their fathers.
9. There are many cities and large towers in Gaul.
10. Everything will be successful for the daring.

Section 24

Grammar : **Regular Comparison of Adjectives.**
R.P. pp. 41, 42 : S.P. p. 24 : P.G. p. 78.

TO EXPRESS COMPARISON

A **Comparative Adjective** may be followed by the **Ablative Case** to express the thing with which another is compared. This is called the **Ablative of Comparison;**

e.g.   *The general was not braver than the king.*
        Imperator rege non fortior erat.

Instead of the Ablative of Comparison we can always use *quam, than.* The two things compared are then always in the same Case ;

e.g.   **Imperator fortior erat quam rex.**

The construction with *quam* must always be used except where the two things compared are expressed by two Nouns and the first of these is in the **Nominative** or **Accusative Case.**

Exercise 76

1. The danger will be more serious for our men.

2. The cavalry will be hindered by a very broad river.

3. The city was very beautiful.

4. The bravest soldiers held the right wing.

5. I have avoided the most serious dangers.

6. The infantry were more successful than the cavalry.

7. The attack of the enemy was very fierce.

8. The general drew up the boldest soldiers opposite the town.

9. Many burdens hinder a soldier.

10. Large cities are not always very beautiful.

Exercise 77

1. Our men have overcome the Gauls by a very fierce attack.

2. The infantry will be braver than the cavalry in the battle.

3. The towers of the Gauls were higher than their walls.

4. We were hindered by a very broad river.

5. The burdens of the Roman citizens were very heavy.

6. The Belgians fortified their towns by very high walls.

7. The plan of the general is bolder.

8. The wall (is) very high, the river is very broad.

9. Nothing is more beautiful than wisdom.

10. The Romans are not more daring than the Belgians.

Exercise 78

1. The bravest leader is not always the most successful.

2. The Gaul's arms were heavier than (those) of our men.

3. We fiercely attacked the cavalry of the Belgians.

4. The line was drawn up opposite a very deep river.

5. The boldest generals are always loved by their soldiers.

6. You will not be more daring than your father.

7. The town was fortified by a high rampart and a broad river.

8. We shall avoid the more serious dangers of war.

9. The camp was attacked by the brave general.

10. The broadest rivers are not always the deepest.

SECTION 25

Grammar : **Comparison of Adjectives in *-ilis*, and Irregular Comparison.** R.P. p. 42 : S.P. p. 25 : P.G. pp. 80–1.

Exercise 79

1. He had easily avoided the greatest dangers.
2. The towns of the barbarians were very small.
3. The Gauls had larger weapons than our men.
4. War is a very easy matter to a Roman.
5. The greatest dangers never terrify a brave man.
6. The camp of the Belgians is smaller than (that) of the Romans.
7. The plan of the general is better than (that) of the citizens.
8. Our men had better arms than the enemy.
9. The Gauls had very good horses.
10. It was an easy matter for the Roman army.

Exercise 80

1. He drew up the best soldiers opposite the rampart.
2. The largest cities are not always the most beautiful.
3. The best citizens will not neglect the king's advice.
4. The town was fortified by very large towers.
5. The line of the Romans was smaller than (that) of the barbarians.
6. The plan of the general will be very useful for the army.
7. The shields of the enemy were very small.
8. We had never attacked a larger camp.
9. Labienus was liked by the best soldiers.
10. With the greatest courage you have overcome all dangers.

Exercise 81

1. The most fierce attacks are not always the most successful.
2. The best soldiers have been led back into camp.
3. Our men seized the town with great valour.
4. The cavalry easily overcame the enemy's forces.
5. A small number of infantry was attacked by our men.
6. The soldiers had fought well against the barbarians.
7. Our men withstood the attack with great courage.
8. The Gauls fiercely attacked the Roman infantry.
9. We shall easily overcome the forces of Belgians.
10. The boy had been well advised by his father.

SECTION 26

Grammar : **1st and 2nd Persons ; 3rd Person,** *is, ea, id.*
R.P. pp. 48, 49 : S.P. pp. 30, 31 : P.G. p. 97.

PERSONAL PRONOUNS

Latin has no 3rd Person Pronoun like *he, she, it.* It uses
Demonstratives instead, most frequently **is, ea, id ;**

  e.g. *I love my country : I will save it.*
      Patriam amo : eam servabo.

Remember that the Personal Pronoun is not usually
expressed when it is the subject of a Verb. It should be
expressed where there is emphasis or a contrast;

  e.g. *You love your country : we saved it.*
      Vos patriam amatis: nos servavimus.

REFLEXIVE PRONOUNS

A Reflexive is a Pronoun used in an Oblique Case, and
standing for the same person as the subject of its sentence.

In the 1st and 2nd Persons the Personal Pronouns are used
as Reflexives ;

  e.g. **Te celas.**
      You are hiding yourself.

In the 3rd Person there is a special Reflexive, viz. **se** (both
Singular and Plural) ;

  e.g. **Milites se celant.**
      The soldiers are hiding themselves.

Grammar : 1st **Person,** *meus, noster ;* 2nd **Person,** *tuus,*
vester ; 3rd **Person,** *suus* [**Reflexive only**].
R.P. p. 49 : S.P. p. 31 : P.G. p. 98.

POSSESSIVE ADJECTIVES

The words called Possessive Pronouns are all *Adjectives,* and
must agree with the Noun to which they belong ;

e.g.   *Your father saved our city.*
          Tuus pater nostram urbem servavit.[1]

For the 3rd Person the Adjective **suus** is only to be used
Reflexively, i.e. referring to the subject of its sentence ;

e.g.   *The Gauls laid waste their own fields.*
          Galli suos agros vastaverunt.

When *his, their,* etc., are not Reflexive, we must use the
Genitives of *is, ea, id* ;   e.g.

Galli Germanos oppugnant et tecta eorum incendunt.
The Gauls attack the Germans and set fire to their houses
     (i.e. the houses of the Germans).

N.B.—It will be obvious from the above rule that *his, their,* etc.,
cannot be Reflexive when they qualify the subject of the sentence ;

e.g.   *His father heard him.*
          Eius pater eum audivit.

---

[1] It is not usually necessary to express the Possessive Adjective in
Latin when it is of the same person as the subject of the sentence ;

e.g.   *I love my father.*   **Patrem amo.**
       I love your father.   **Tuum patrem amo.**

Exercise 82

1. My plan was better than yours.

2. Your victory was announced to me.

3. Our soldiers attacked their town.

4. We have announced the victory to him.

5. I shall not hide myself in the city.

6. The citizens have saved their own city.

7. The cavalry hid themselves in the wood.

8. The barbarians have laid waste our fields.

9. We shall not be terrified by the attack of your infantry.

10. His plan was very useful to the citizens.

Exercise 83

1. We announced the battle to you.

2. The Gauls bravely withstood our attack.

3. Their city was well fortified by a high rampart.

4. Our country will never be ruled by barbarians.

5. The enemy were overcome by me.

6. We shall not neglect the advice of your general.

7. The enemies' soldiers are hiding themselves in the woods.

8. Your army will be hindered by the river.

9. His son was not wounded by the arrow.

10. Our cavalry had been drawn up on the right wing.

Exercise 84

1. The heaviest burdens will easily be carried by us.

2. The king will hear you and save the city.

3. The advice of my son was very useful to me.

4. The affair will be very difficult for you and your citizens.

5. Nothing is more beautiful than our city.

6. It will be easier for you than for us.

7. He saved himself by his own stratagem.

8. Their cavalry are braver than their infantry.

9. The rivers of our country are very broad and deep.

10. Their camp was smaller than ours.

Grammar : hic **and** ille. R.P. p. 49 : S.P. p. 31 :
P.G. p. 102.

DEMONSTRATIVE PRONOUNS

N.B.—**Hic** is used like the English *this* for what is near to the speaker
in place or time ;

> e.g. *This city (where I am).*
> **Haec urbs.**

Ille is used like *that* for what is farther away ;

> e.g. *This tower is not higher than that yonder.*
> **Haec turris non altior est illā.**

Exercise 85

1. Nothing will be more useful to our citizens than your
plan.

2. This part of the city has not been fortified.

3. We shall lead our soldiers into that town.

4. The dangers of this war will be very serious.

5. Your soldiers assailed this tower.

6. Their cavalry were hidden in this wood.

7. That danger will be overcome by our leaders.

8. The greatest wars are not feared by those barbarians.

9. That horse has been wounded by an arrow.

10. This battle was very fortunate for our troops.

Exercise 86

1. This city was built by the Gauls.
2. This sea is very deep.
3. The general saved himself, but not his country.
4. These attacks are easily withstood by the brave soldiers.
5. Their weapons were wounding our horses.
6. You will not frighten the brave citizens by this device.
7. This part of the city was held by Labienus.
8. These soldiers were drawn up on the left wing.
9. The barbarians will never overcome this army.
10. You will not save yourself by this plan.

Exercise 87

1. This victory was announced to us by the captives.
2. That advice will never be neglected by me.
3. These arms were carried by my father.
4. The dangers of war will never terrify these citizens.
5. This thing will be easy to me and to you.
6. This most beautiful city was attacked by the enemy.
7. Those fields were laid waste by the Belgians.
8. The victory was announced to me by this boy.
9. These shields are very broad and very heavy.
10. These cities were fortified by high ramparts and towers.

Section 27

Grammar : ipse and *idem.* R.P. p. 50 : S.P. p. 32 : P.G. pp. 98, 102.

Self in the **Nominative always**, and **in the Oblique Cases when not Reflexive**, is expressed by **ipse ;**

e.g. *I myself heard it.*
Ipse audivi.

He was praised by Caesar himself.
A Caesare ipso laudatus est.

Exercise 88

1. The soldiers themselves were terrified by the enemy.

2. The soldiers saved themselves by the same plan.

3. They will attack our city themselves.

4. The same things are not easy to all men.

5. The burden itself was not very heavy.

6. The same part of the city was being attacked by the infantry.

7. The Belgians themselves do not fear our soldiers.

8. The wisdom of the same general saved the town.

9. We announced the victory to the general himself.

10. Both cavalry and infantry were overcome by the same enemy.

Exercise 89

1. You praise yourself; you do not praise your soldiers.

2. His army was defeated by the same enemy.

3. The son himself is more daring than his father.

4. This camp was attacked by the same troops.

5. The general had drawn up all the cavalry on the same wing.

6. We were fighting bravely opposite the same rampart.

7. These serious dangers are feared by all the citizens.

8. Both the cavalry and the infantry were praised by the same general.

9. Their leaders bravely withstood our attacks.

10. War itself is not a serious danger.

Exercise 90

1. The wretched captives were saved by their own device.

2. We hid ourselves in the same wood.

3. This land is loved by me, that (one) by you.

4. The king himself was not terrified by fear of war.

5. In the same part of the city the shouts of the enemy were heard.

6. That (thing) itself will not be feared by a brave man.

7. His horse was wounded by the same arrow.

8. The general himself avoided all the dangers of the war.

9. The same river was both very broad and very deep.

10. The general will draw up his cavalry on the left wing.

Section 28

Grammar : R.P. p. 51 : S.P. p. 32 : P.G. p. 104.

RELATIVE PRONOUNS

In *I saw the gate : this was open,* we have two separate sentences. In the second *this* is a Demonstrative Pronoun standing for *the gate* in the first, and it would be parsed as having the same Gender and Number as *gate.* But its Case has nothing to do with *gate ;* it is the Subject of *was,* and is therefore in the Nominative Case.

In *I saw the gate, which was open,* we say the same thing, but in place of the Demonstrative *this* we use the Relative *which,* because it serves to connect the sentences. Here *which* stands for *gate* just as *this* did, and for the same reasons it must have the same Gender and Number as *gate,* but gets its Case from its own clause. The word *gate* is called its Antecedent.

Therefore in Latin as in English we have the rule :

A Relative Pronoun agrees with its Antecedent in Gender, Number, and Person, but its Case depends on its relation to its own clause.

> e.g. *I praised the soldier, who had fought bravely.*
> **Militem laudavi qui bene pugnaverat.**
> *The wall, which we built, was very high.*
> **Murus, quem aedificavimus, altissimus erat.**
> *This is Gaius, whose son I was praising.*
> **Hic est Gaius cuius filium laudabam.**

If you are ever in doubt as to the Case of the Relative, turn the clause into one with a Demonstrative or Personal Pronoun. The above could only be " I praised the soldier. *He* had fought bravely." " This is Gaius. I was praising *his* (Lat. **eius)** son." Remember that the Relative stands for these Demonstratives or Personal Pronouns, and must have the same Case that they would have.

N.B.—The Relative can never be omitted in Latin as it often is in English.
The second of the above sentences could in English be " The wall we built was very high." This is impossible in Latin.

ELE - F

Exercise 91

1. The ship which we built was very large.

2. The camp which they attacked was smaller than their own.

3. The man who announced the victory was praised by the general.

4. The part of the city which we neglected was attacked by the enemy.

5. The men whom you rule do not like you.

6. The soldiers were terrified by the shouts which they heard.

7. We were attacked by the enemy, who had always feared us.

8. The wall which we built was higher than (that) of the Gauls.

9. Citizens do not like a general who is always defeated.

10. The ships which we are building will avoid all dangers.

Exercise 92

1. The soldiers whom we had praised were defeated.

2. I, who have never avoided danger, shall be your leader.

3. The gods, whom we fear, will hear us.

4. In this city, which we were attacking, there were many captives.

5. The general himself, whom all loved, was wounded.

6. We seized the city, which had been fortified by a high rampart.

7. They will never defeat us who defeated their fathers.

8. Many things which frighten barbarians do not frighten us.

9. The soldiers who were holding the town fought fiercely.

10. Cotta led his troops into the fields which had been ravaged by the enemy.

Exercise 93

1. This victory was announced by a soldier who had avoided the battle.

2. The town we were attacking had been fortified with towers and ramparts.

3. We shall not neglect the advice of the general who defeated the enemy.

4. The ships we had built were larger than (those) of the Gauls.

5. This burden, which you are carrying, is very heavy.

6. The general we loved was defeated by the Gauls.

7. Wisdom is very useful to men.

8. The same army had defeated Labienus.

9. We shall fortify the city which we are building.

10. This camp is larger than (that) which you were attacking.

Exercise 94

1. The general, by whose arrival the city was saved, was wounded himself.

2. The man to whom you announced the victory announced it to me.

3. This custom, which you praise, I blame.

4. The cavalry, by whose valour the city was saved, were praised by the general.

5. All whose fathers fought against the Gauls will fight bravely now.

6. This was the king whose troops we overcame.

7. The army which you led back into camp had never been defeated.

8. The wood in which we hid our men was very large.

9. Nothing will be more useful to us than this plan.

10. The country which we love we will save by our valour.

Exercise 95

1. You will not be terrified by the arrival of larger forces.

2. The soldiers' hearts were emboldened by the victory.

3. We withstood the attack of the enemy who assailed us.

4. The bravest men had been placed on the right wing.

5. The same city was held by smaller forces of Romans.

6. The gods rule the plans of men.

7. The general by his arrival emboldened the hearts of the soldiers.

8. The shouts of the barbarians were heard in our camp.

9. The arrival of these troops emboldened the hearts of our men.

10. To a soldier nothing is more useful than his arms.

Exercise 96

1. The enemy were terrified by the arrival of the general who had often defeated them.

2. We all praised the general by whose valour the town had been saved.

3. The Romans, whose customs all praise, were not often defeated.

4. Labienus, who had been warned by us, was wounded by the enemy.

5. The river by which we were hindered was very deep.

6. That part of the city which the enemy attacked had been neglected by us.

7. Your sons will rule the land in which you are now fighting

8. All blamed the general by whose advice we had fortified the city.

9. The town in which we hid the captives is now held by the enemy.

10. The Gauls built the town, the walls of which we are attacking.

SECTION 29

Grammar: **Cardinal Numerals, 1-20.** R.P. pp. 45, 46, 47 : S.P. pp. 27, 28, 29 : P.G. pp. 84, 86.

TO EXPRESS *PLACE*

Place is generally expressed by phrases with Prepositions :

(1) **Place to which** motion is directed by **ad** or **in** with the **Accusative.**

(2) **Place from which** motion proceeds by **ab** or **ex**[1] with the **Ablative.**

(3) **Place at which** anything happens by **in** with the **Ablative.**

The important exceptions to this will be given in the next rule (p. 74).

e.g.

He marches out of Italy into the territories of the Gauls.
Ex Italia in agros Gallorum contendit.

He was sent to me and remained in the city.
Ad me missus est et in urbe mansit.

---

[1] Where *from* is equal to *out of* use **ex.**

Exercise 97

1. He sent seven cohorts out of the camp.

2. Caesar marched from Italy into the territories of the Gauls.

3. The legions which we sent were defeated.

4. The soldiers of this legion do not fear the enemy.

5. One cohort was hindered by the river.

6. This legion was attacked by the enemy's cavalry.

7. Caesar will send five cohorts into the town.

8. We shall march out of the camp into Italy.

9. The soldiers of that legion will remain in the camp.

10. Two armies of the enemy were marching to the town.

Exercise 98

1. The soldiers brought twenty captives to Caesar.

2. The cavalry of two legions will remain in the wood.

3. Larger forces were sent by the general to Gaul.

4. There were in Gaul eight towns which we had not attacked.

5. The three legions which you sent have been defeated.

6. Two cohorts will be drawn up opposite the rampart.

7. Caesar praised the soldiers of that legion.

8. We shall place four cohorts on the left wing.

9. The enemy were defeated by the valour of this legion.

10. Eight cohorts have been sent into the town.

Exercise 99

1. The soldiers of one cohort avoided all risks.

2. A Roman army has been sent into the territories of the Gauls.

3. Two boys announced the victory to us.

4. The barbarians withstood the attack of the three cohorts.

5. One legion which they have sent has been defeated.

6. Wise men will not neglect the advice of the gods.

7. The camp was fortified by three ramparts.

8. There were fifteen captives in the town.

9. They have sent to us a large number of soldiers.

10. Five legions were marching from Italy to Gaul.

SECTION 30

TO EXPRESS *PLACE* (*continued*)

With the **proper names** of **towns** and **small islands** and also with the two words **domus** and **rus**—

1. **Place to which** is expressed by the Accusative, and **Place from which** by the Ablative, but **without a Preposition** ;

    e.g.   *He sailed from Rhodes to Athens.*
             Rhodo Athenas navigavit.

2. **Place at which** is expressed by the **Locative Case.**

The Locative was a Case meant to express " place where " but was only partly preserved in Latin. Its forms are the same as those of the Ablative except in the Singular of the 1st and 2nd Declensions, where they are the same as those of the Genitive ; e.g.

Romae	*at Rome*	(Nom. **Roma**).
Rhodi	*at Rhodes*	(Nom. **Rhodus**).
Athenis	*at Athens*	(Nom. pl. **Athenae**).
Gadibus	*at Cadiz*	(Nom. pl. **Gades**).
Carthagine		
(or **Carthagini**)	*at Carthage*	(Nom. **Carthago**).

So **domi**, *at home*, **ruri** or **rure** *in the country.*

Exercise 100

1. We marched from Rome to the territories of the Gauls.

2. At Athens all feared the arrival of the enemy.

3. Many ships will sail to Athens.

4. The soldiers whom we defeated at Cadiz will not fight again.

5. The general brought all the captives to Rome.

6. At Rome the advice of Caesar had been neglected.

7. The men whom we saw at Rome are marching to Athens.

8. The boy who remained in the camp announced the victory of the enemy.

9. The barbarians were defeated by the Romans at Carthage.

10. His father had been wounded by an arrow at Cadiz.

Exercise 101

1. He marched with three legions to Carthage.

2. The citizens who remained at Athens were blamed by the general.

3. The danger will be more serious at Rome than at Carthage.

4. The barbarians wounded the king himself with an arrow.

5. In Athens all men praise wisdom.

6. Two cohorts are remaining at Cadiz.

7. Three towns had been seized by the enemy.

8. Caesar marched into the territories of the Gauls with all his forces.

9. There is a large number of citizens at Rome.

10. By your valour you have again saved your country.

Exercise 102

1. There are in Cadiz two legions who have never been defeated.

2. The soldiers whom Labienus sent announced the victory to us.

3. There are at Rome the best soldiers and the bravest generals.

4. We shall never see a more beautiful city.

5. My father sailed with three ships from Athens to Rhodes.

6. The shouts of the barbarians were heard in Rome by all the citizens.

7. The city which we saw has been fortified with a rampart.

8. We shall march with one legion to Carthage.

9. Larger forces of the enemy are marching to Rome.

10. The river which you saw is very broad and very deep.

SECTION 31

Grammar : **Ordinal Numbers, 1-20.** R.P. pp. 46, 47 :
S.P. pp. 28, 29 : P.G. p. 84.

TO EXPRESS *TIME*

(1) The length of time **during which** an action lasts is
expressed by the **Accusative** Case without a Preposition ; e.g.

They were fortifying the city twenty years (for, during,
throughout twenty years).
Viginti annos urbem muniebant.

(2) The time **at which** a thing happens or the limit of time
within which it happens is expressed by the **Ablative** Case
without a Preposition ;

e.g.   *On the fifth day he was set free.*
Quinto die liberatus est.

Within five days he was set free.
Quinque diebus liberatus est.

N.B.—This last is sometimes confused with the "length of time"
expressed by the Accusative. But remember that when the Accusative
is used the action is represented as going on *throughout the whole time,*
when the Ablative is used it is represented as happening *at a certain
point within the period.*

He was sailing for five days=**Quinque dies navigabat.**
Within five days he set sail=**Quinque diebus navigavit.**

Exercise 103

1. The captives will be set free in three days.

2. On that day the sixth legion marched to Rome.

3. One cohort fought with the enemy for five hours.

4. In the same year the city was seized by the Gauls.

5. His father remained at Carthage for three years.

6. In a few years the city will have been fortified with walls.

7. For many hours we were attacking the line of the enemy.

8. The men whom we saw at Carthage remained for a few days.

9. On the same day the tenth legion was led into the territories of the Gauls.

10. In the third year the Gauls were defeated by their enemies.

Exercise 104

1. On that day the cries of the barbarians were heard in the city.

2. The captives whom we saw will be set free in a few days.

3. For very many days there was a serious danger of war.

4. On the sixth day we saw the same men again.

5. At the sixth hour the army was led back into camp.

6. For three hours the tenth legion fought with the enemy.

7. The soldier by whose valour the town was saved has been set free.

8. On the tenth day we sailed from Athens to Italy.

9. The soldiers of the fifth legion were laying waste the fields.

10. The general to whom we reported the victory has been sent to Rome.

Exercise 105

1. In the tenth year the enemy were defeated.

2. For a few days we shall remain at Athens with our father.

3. The barbarians are marching to Rome with huge forces.

4. On the fourth day the king led his forces into the city.

5. The fifth legion, which was marching to Carthage, was hindered by a river.

6. For two hours our men fought bravely with the enemy.

7. The boy whom we have sent will report the battle in five days.

8. On the third day the town was seized by the Belgians.

9. The tenth legion, by whose valour the enemy were defeated, was praised by Caesar.

10. We ourselves saw the man on the same day.

SECTION 32

Grammar : **Imperative Active of Regular Verbs and of sum.** R.P. pp. 63, 65, 67, 69, 71 : S.P. pp. 41, 43, 44, 45, 46 : P.G. pp. 125, 129, 133, 137, 153.

THE IMPERATIVE MOOD

N.B.—The longer forms given in the Grammar are not to be used in the following exercises. The only forms wanted are

Active	2nd Sing.	**ama**	2nd Plu.	**amate**
Passive	2nd Sing.	**amare**	2nd Plu.	**amamini**

and the corresponding forms in the other Conjugations.

Exercise 106

1. Hide yourselves, citizens : the enemy have seized the town.

2. Free the captives, Commius : they have saved the state.

3. You remain at Carthage : I shall march to Rome.

4. Be brave, soldiers : we have always defeated these men.

5. Praise the valour of your fathers, citizens.

6. Hold the city with a few cavalry.

7. Fortify the walls with three ramparts and a high tower.

8. Rule yourself : men who rule themselves are praised by all.

9. Fight bravely : the tenth legion is marching to us.

10. Lay waste your fields, citizens : the Romans will not have corn.

Exercise 107

1. Set free the hostages : the Gauls are not preparing war.
2. Love your country and your king, boys.
3. Avoid all dangers : the rivers of this land are very deep.
4. Send the fifth legion to Gaul, (and) the sixth to Carthage.
5. Withstand the fiercest attacks of the enemy bravely.
6. Remain in the city for three days : the danger is serious.
7. Defeat the enemy whom we have already defeated.
8. Send five cohorts to Cadiz.
9. Fortify the camp with a high rampart.
10. Hold the city with five cohorts : send more men to us.

Exercise 108

1. Sail to Rhodes with four ships : carry corn to our soldiers.
2. Draw up the cavalry on the left wing.
3. The hostages which were sent by the Belgians were set free by Caesar.
4. The state which our fathers saved shall never be ruled by barbarians.
5. The battle, in which the fourth legion had fought, was reported at Rome.
6. On the same day twenty hostages were set free.
7. Many states had not sent corn to Caesar.
8. We shall not again see that most beautiful city.
9. The general himself remained in the town with a few cohorts.
10. The citizens of this state had never seen a Roman army.

SECTION 33

Grammar: **Comparison of Adverbs.** R.P. p. 44 : S.P. p. 26 :
P.G. p. 96. **Imperative Passive of Regular Verbs.**
R.P. pp. 73, 75, 77, 79 : S.P. pp. 51, 53, 55, 57 :
P.G. pp. 127, 131, 135, 139.

Exercise 109

1. Be advised by your father : he will advise you better than this man.

2. We shall fight more bravely than the Gauls.

3. Fear the gods : be feared by men.

4. The Gauls were building larger ships.

5. The fifth legion fought most bravely on that day.

6. For a few hours the enemy withstood our attack more bravely.

7. Be feared by the barbarians, Romans.

8. We shall defeat the soldiers of this state more easily.

9. The same part of the city was held by the fifth legion.

10. The town itself was not known to our general.

Exercise 110

1. All the nations of Gaul feared Caesar.

2. Be advised by me ; avoid the risk.

3. Our men fought very fiercely for three hours.

4. Your father has advised you very well.

5. Never had the cavalry fought more bravely than on that day.

6. We defeated the forces of the Gauls very easily.

7. Be praised by all men : praise is always welcome.

8. Withstand their attacks more bravely.

9. That part of the land was known to few men.

10. The eighth legion marched on the same day to Gaul.

Exercise 111

1. The citizens, who had been warned by us, very easily withstood the enemy's attack.

2. The cavalry fought more bravely than the infantry.

3. Be ruled by the advice of your general : fortify the city.

4. The king of this state had not sent corn to Caesar.

5. We shall send hostages to the enemy.

6. The Romans fought most bravely by land and by sea.

7. The enemy's weapons were more heavy than our shields.

8. Nothing is more welcome to us than your advice.

9. The voice of the king himself was heard in the city.

10. Two legions fought most bravely on behalf of their country.

SECTION 34

Grammar : **Infinitive Active of Regular Verbs and of *sum*.**
R.P. pp. 63, 65, 67, 69, 71 : S.P. pp. 41, 43, 45, 47,
49 : P.G. pp. 125, 129, 133, 137, 153.

THE INFINITIVE

In the sentence *Seeing is believing* we have instances of
what we call Verbal Nouns, i.e. Nouns which express the
action of the Verb. We should parse *seeing* as a Noun, the
Subject of *is*, and *believing* as a Noun, the Complement of *is*
(see p. 52).

From every English Verb we can form a Verbal Noun
ending in *-ing*. But we can always use the Infinitive instead,
e.g. the above sentence might be *To see is to believe.* This
shows that the Infinitive is a Verbal Noun as much as the
Noun in *-ing*.

The Latin Infinitive has precisely the same use. **The
Infinitive is a Verbal Noun and as such it can be the
Subject or Complement of a Verb, most frequently of est.**

e.g.   *To work is to pray (working is praying).*
        Laborare est orare.

[*Laborare* is the Subject, *orare* the Complement of *est.*]

        It is an evil to err.
        Errare malum est.

[The Latin literally means *To err is an evil,* and *errare* is
the Subject of *est.*]

Exercise 112

1. It was easier to conquer the Gauls than the Romans.

2. It will be difficult to carry on war for three years.

3. Fighting will be more welcome to the soldiers than to the citizens.

4. It will be most useful to our state to have conquered these enemies.

5. It was a splendid thing to have defeated so large a number of Gauls.

6. In three years it will be more easy to carry on war.

7. It is pleasant to fight on behalf of our country and citizens.

8. It was the custom of the Romans to carry on war by land and sea.

9. It will be very easy to hear the general's voice.

10. It will be better to hide the cavalry in the woods.

Exercise 113

1. It will be most useful to us to have laid waste the enemy's fields.

2. It is better to conquer by courage than by stratagem.

3. It was the custom of this nation to fortify their towns with high walls.

4. To send forces to Gaul will be easier than to fight in Italy.

5. It is better to withstand the attack than to have avoided danger.

6. The ninth legion will be sent this year to Carthage.

7. It will be very difficult to fortify that part of the city.

8. It is a splendid thing to have withstood the attack of the enemy.

9. The Romans have carried on war by land and sea for many years.

10. A campaign was conducted by Caesar against the Gauls.

Exercise 114

1. The Gauls, against whom we had conducted a campaign, conquered us.

2. The fifth legion, which was sent to Gaul, has been conquered.

3. It is often more easy to praise than to blame.

4. It is most pleasing to me to see so large a number of citizens.

5. The soldiers whom we sent to Gaul carried on war for many years.

6. In a few years it will be easy to carry corn to the city.

7. It was most difficult to avoid so great a danger.

8. It is a bad (thing) to have neglected a good general's advice.

9. It will be very easy to have conquered the enemy.

10. It was the custom of the Romans to fortify all their camps with ramparts.

SECTION 35

Grammar : **Infinitive Passive of Regular Verbs.**
R.P. pp. 73, 75, 77, 79 : S.P. pp. 51, 53, 55, 57 :
P.G. pp. 127, 131, 135, 139.

Exercise 115

1. It is easier to be blamed than to be praised.

2. It will be a good thing for these men to be conquered by the Romans.

3. It is an evil to be ruled by bad kings.

4. It will be a serious thing to be attacked by so great a number of barbarians.

5. It is most disgraceful to be terrified by the arrival of the enemy.

6. It will be pleasant to be led back into camp.

7. It was difficult to be heard by all the citizens.

8. Be advised by us : it is better to be advised than to be conquered.

9. It will be very difficult for our men to avoid the arrows of the enemy.

10. It is more disgraceful to be praised by this man than to be blamed by that (one).

Exercise 116

1. Our men were confused by the arrival of the Gauls.

2. Praise those who have conquered the enemies of the state.

3. You have fought most bravely : you have never been conquered.

4. It is most easy to be praised by the base.

5. The camp, which we had fortified, was attacked for three hours.

6. In a few days you will be in a city which I have never seen.

7. The soldiers marched through the territories of the Gauls.

8. It is not disgraceful to be conquered by so large a number of enemies.

9. It is easier to carry on war by land than by sea.

10. It will be more disgraceful to remain in the city than to be defeated.

Exercise 117

1. Send larger forces to us in a few days.

2. In ten days we shall see the general who conquered the Gauls.

3. The Gauls will carry on the war more bravely this year.

4. The plan of the general was to attack the enemy's camp.

5. It is easier to prepare war than to defeat the enemy.

6. The ninth legion, which was sent to Gaul, had never been defeated.

7. It will be very difficult to march through these fields.

8. The leader of the barbarians was defeated by a stratagem.

9. In the same year the citizens of this town built a wall.

10. For five hours we remained in the smaller camp.

SECTION 36

Grammar : **Active Participles of Regular Verbs.**
R.P. pp. 65, 67, 69, 71 : S.P. pp. 43, 45, 47, 49 :
P.G. pp. 125, 129, 133, 137.

PARTICIPLES

A Participle is a Verbal Adjective, and always agrees, like an Adjective, with some Substantive expressed or understood.

In the sentence *I saw a brown horse* we parse *brown* as an Adjective qualifying *horse.*

In *I saw a galloping horse* (or *I saw a horse galloping*) and *I saw a tethered horse* we parse *galloping* and *tethered* as Participles, i.e. forms of Verbs. Yet it is obvious that *galloping* and *tethered* qualify *horse* just as *brown* did in the first sentence —in other words, they are Adjectives in character.

That Participles are also Verbs is clear from the fact that they always express the action of some Verb, and (when Active) can govern an object ; e.g. *I saw a horse drawing a cart.*

Hence we speak of them as Verbal Adjectives.

Latin has the following Participles :

1. The **Present Participle Active,** which represents an action as **still going on** at any time. It corresponds to the English Participle in *-ing* ;

e.g. *I saw a horse running.*
Equum vidi currentem.

2. The **Future Participle Active,** which represents an action as **about to take place** at any time.

> e.g.   *He was about to sail to Athens.*
> **Athenas navigaturus erat.**

Note that English has no Future Participle, and is obliged to render the Latin by such phrases as "about to sail."

3. The **Perfect Participle Passive,** which represents an action as **already completed** at any time.

> e.g.   *Having been wounded he is carried out of the battle.*
> **Vulneratus e proelio portatur.**
>
> *The wounded general we carried out of the battle.*
> **Vulneratum ducem e proelio portavimus.**

N.B.—It is important to notice that Latin has no Perfect Participle *Active* like the English "*having freed* his slave," "*having lost* his money." The form of the sentence must be changed to express these in Latin. This will be explained later.

The Latin Participle can often be used to express a longer English phrase or clause. It is necessary to learn to recognize these. In the following exercises imitate these sentences :

He was killed $\begin{cases} \textit{while} \text{ fighting.} \\ \textit{while he was} \text{ fighting.} \end{cases}$

Pugnans necatus est.

He attacked the enemy $\begin{cases} \textit{when} \text{ already thrown into confusion.} \\ \textit{when they were} \text{ already thrown into} \\ \quad \text{confusion.} \end{cases}$

Jam perturbatos hostes oppugnavit.

N.B.—In the following exercises the words (like *while* and *when* in the above sentences) which do not need separate expression in Latin are printed in italics.

Exercise 118

1. Our men, *while* fortifying their camp, were fiercely attacked by the Gauls.

2. The Romans, *while* hastening to the city, were hindered by a broad river.

3. *While* sailing to Athens we saw the enemy's ships.

4. We saw the boys working in the fields.

5. I fear the general *when he is* blaming me.

6. The Romans were about to lay waste the fields of the Gauls.

7. *While* fighting at Carthage he was wounded by an arrow.

8. We saw a boy running to the wood.

9. The Gauls, *while* attacking our camp, were themselves attacked.

10. *While* freeing the captives he praised their courage.

Exercise 119

1. The tenth legion was about to attack the enemy's camp.

2. *While* setting free the hostages he was killed by his own soldiers.

3. We saw the barbarians hiding arms in the woods.

4. At the fifth hour of the day he marched against the enemy.

5. The enemy, *while* fighting most bravely, were attacked by our cavalry.

6. We were about to carry on war in Gaul.

7. Our men, *while* attacking the camp, were wounded by the enemy's darts.

8. It is disgraceful to kill the men by whom we were saved.

9. Run to the city : announce the victory to the citizens.

10. The men whom we saw in the wood ran to the city.

Exercise 120

1. *While* drawing up his line of battle he was killed by an arrow.

2. There are in this state twenty men who have never seen the king.

3. We attacked the enemy *while they were* carrying corn into the city.

4. The Gauls attacked Labienus *when he was* leading his men into camp.

5. The enemy were about to draw up their line of battle.

6. He was wounded by an arrow *while* leading his men out of the battle.

7. He was about to send larger forces to the city.

8. It is better to be killed than to be conquered.

9. We announced the victory to him *while he was* hastening out of the city.

10. *While* marching through the territories of the Gauls we saw a very broad river.

SECTION 37

Grammar : **Passive Participles of Regular Verbs.**
R.P. pp. 73, 75, 77, 79 : S.P. pp. 51, 53, 55, 57 :
P.G. pp. 127, 131, 135, 139.

Exercise 121

1. We attacked the Gauls *when* hindered by the river.

2. We conquered the enemy *when they had been* terrified
by the arrival of Caesar.

3. They killed the captives *when they had been* condemned.

4. We attacked a city fortified by a high wall.

5. For three days Labienus held the city with a few troops.

6. We set free the prisoners *who had been* neglected by the
soldiers.

7. The cavalry, hidden in the woods, were defeated by our
men.

8. This city, preserved by our fathers, we all love.

9. The wounded general was carried into the camp by the
soldiers.

10. In a few years it will not be easy to send corn.

Exercise 122

1. The prisoners, *when* condemned, were killed by the soldiers.

2. Those whom we praise we do not always like.

3. The wall, built by the Gauls, was seen by our fathers.

4. Wounded by an arrow, he ran into the camp.

5. Attacked by the enemy, we fought most bravely for three hours.

6. It will be more easy to attack this city than to conquer the citizens.

7. Blamed by all, he hastened to Rome.

8. Kill the men whom we have condemned.

9. Attack the enemy *while* hindered by this river.

10. It is better to have saved our country than to have avoided danger.

Exercise 123

1. *While* fighting on behalf of their country they were conquered.

2. *While* hindered by the river they were attacked by the Roman cavalry.

3. By the valour of the citizens our city has been set free

4. The best plan will be to send larger forces to the war.

5. Neglected by his own father, he remained in the city.

6. The cohorts which we sent were led by Labienus.

7. They are holding that part of the city which we have often attacked.

8. It is very easy to fight, very difficult to conquer.

9. It is not disgraceful to be condemned by bad men.

10. We were about to send a large army into Gaul.

SECTION 38

Grammar : **Subjunctive Active of Regular Verbs (1st and 2nd Conjugations) and *sum*.** R.P. pp. 63, 65, 67 : S.P. pp. 41, 43, 45 : P.G. pp. 124–5, 128–9, 152–3.

THE SUBJUNCTIVE MOOD

(1) **An Exhortation (1st or 3rd Person),** or a **Wish for the Future,** is expressed by the **Present Subjunctive.** If negative **ne** is used with it.

> e.g. *Let all fear my words.*
> **Omnes verba mea timeant.**
> *Let us not praise evil men.*
> **Ne malos laudemus.**
> *May the citizens be brave.*
> **Sint cives fortes.**

(2) Translate the Conjunction *since* by **cum** with a **Subjunctive Tense.**[1]

If the English has a

Present Tense use the Present Subjunctive.		
Past	,, ,,	Imperfect Subjunctive.
Perfect	,, ,,	Perfect Subjunctive.
Pluperfect	,, ,,	Pluperfect Subjunctive.

---

[1] The introduction of this construction here is anticipating future work. But as practice is required in the formation of all the Subjunctive tenses, this construction has been chosen for the purpose as involving least difficulty to the learner at this stage.

e.g.   Since they *are* allies we will summon all.
       Cum socii *sint* omnes convocabimus.

       Since they *were* allies we summoned all.
       Cum socii *essent* omnes convocavimus.

       Since Caesar *has remained* we are safe.
       Cum Caesar *manserit* tuti sumus.

       Since Caesar *had remained* we were safe.
       Cum Caesar *mansisset* tuti eramus.

Exercise 124

1. Let us avoid all dangers, citizens.

2. Let us not sail to Athens.

3. Build larger ships, Romans.

4. May they be more fortunate than their fathers.

5. Since he fears the enemy, he will remain in the camp.

6. May we not see the enemy in this land.

7. Since he had laid waste the fields of allies, he was blamed by all.

8. Since he was at Rome, he was not condemned.

9. Since you have soldiers, send forces to your allies.

10. Let us withstand their attack and free our country.

Exercise 125

1. May the Romans defeat the Gauls this year.

2. Let us not attack the larger camp.

3. Let me not remain in the camp with the wounded.

4. Since you have freed your country, you will be praised by all.

5. Let us summon all the forces of the allies.

6. Let us build a greater number of ships this year.

7. Let us defeat the enemy whom we have never feared.

8. May he not remain in that city.

9. Let us kill the condemned prisoners.

10. Let us defeat the enemy by our valour.

Exercise 126

1. Let us not blame the good customs of our fathers.

2. May we free the country which we all love.

3. May you fight bravely and defeat the Gauls.

4. Let us not fear a conquered enemy.

5. Let us seize that part of the city.

6. Since he is preparing war, let us attack his camp.

7. May we never see the Roman legions in this city.

8. Since he has remained at Rome he will not fight for his country.

9. Let us carry the wounded men to the camp.

10. Since he was not in the city he did not see the king.

Section 39

Grammar : **Subjunctive Active of Regular Verbs (3rd and 4th Conjugations).** R.P. pp. 69, 71 : S.P. pp. 47, 49 : P.G. pp. 132-3, 136-7.

A command in the negative (i.e. a prohibition) may be expressed by **ne** with the **2nd Person of the Perfect Subjunctive.**

e.g.   *Do not be afraid.*
      Ne timueris.

N.B.—For a more usual way of expressing a prohibition see p. 113.

Exercise 127

1. Let us not neglect the advice of our generals.

2. Do not send the boy to the city.

3. May we conquer the enemy who are terrifying our allies.

4. Let us carry on the war in the territories of the Gauls.

5. Let us send corn to the Roman army.

6. Let us not fear the men whom our fathers conquered.

7. Since the citizens have neglected our advice they will be conquered.

8. Since he had sent troops to the town, he remained in the camp himself.

9. Let us fortify this city with walls and towers.

10. Let us not hear the words of this evil man.

Exercise 128

1. At that time the customs of the Romans were praised by all.

2. Praise the valour of these men who have fought bravely for their country.

3. Let us on this day conquer the enemy who have killed our general.

4. Since we have conquered this nation we shall hasten to Rome.

5. Since they had not sent hostages Caesar summoned their leaders.

6. Let us not hinder the victory of our men.

7. Let us send an army to that state.

8. Let us not neglect those by whose valour we were saved.

9. Since he is carrying on war in Gaul, he will not be sent to Carthage.

10. Let us draw up our line of battle opposite the city.

Exercise 129

1. Since he was attacking the camp, he did not see our men.

2. It was the custom of the Romans to carry the wounded out of the battle.

3. At that time the enemy were holding our city.

4. The Gauls have withstood our attacks most bravely.

5. It is most disgraceful to condemn a man whom all praise.

6. Let us lead back our conquered soldiers into the camp.

7. Let all the states send corn to Caesar.

8. Since the tenth legion is afraid, all are afraid.

9. Let us hinder the Romans *while* fortifying their camp.

10. At that time we had both ships and soldiers.

SECTION 40

Grammar : **Subjunctive Passive of Regular Verbs (1st and 2nd Conjugations).** R.P. pp. 73, 75 : S.P. pp. 51, 53 : P.G. pp. 126–7, 130–1.

Exercise 130

1. Let us not be terrified by a conquered enemy.

2. May we always be loved by our allies.

3. Since he has been wounded, he will not fight again.

4. Since the city had been preserved, the citizens were not afraid.

5. Let the heaviest burdens be carried by the soldiers.

6. Since the victory had been announced, they ran to the city.

7. We are all in the city, since the enemy are laying waste our fields.

8. Since all things have been prepared, let us hasten to the city.

9. Let a meeting be held in three days.

10. May the enemy be defeated by our cavalry.

Exercise 131

1. May the city be preserved by the valour of our men.

2. Let meetings be held at the same time in Rome.

3. Let us not be frightened by an enemy whom our fathers defeated.

4. Since the wall has now been built, we do not fear the enemy.

5. Let us not be thrown into confusion by the arrival of Caesar.

6. Since they had withstood our attack, we summoned a meeting.

7. Let the wounded be carried out of the battle.

8. Since our leaders have been killed, we shall not remain.

9. Let us praise those who rule us well.

10. Do not remain : the enemy have drawn up their line.

Exercise 132

1. They have set free the hostages whom we sent.

2. For many years this state carried on war with the Romans.

3. Since the tenth legion had been defeated, we summoned a meeting.

4. Since part of the Roman army had been seen by the enemy, the barbarians were terrified.

5. Let him be condemned himself, since he has set free the prisoners.

6. He was afraid, since he had never seen a Roman army.

7. Let us attack the enemy at the fourth hour.

8. Hold meetings, citizens : free your country.

9. Let the captives, whom we sent, be killed.

10. He had conducted a campaign in Gaul most successfully for many years.

SECTION 41

Grammar : **Subjunctive Passive of Regular Verbs (3rd and 4th Conjugations).** R.P. pp. 77, 79 : S.P. pp. 55, 57 : P.G. pp. 134–5, 138–9.

Exercise 133

1. May the words of our fathers be heard by all.

2. Since the city has now been fortified, the citizens are preparing war.

3. Let us not send help to the enemies of our state.

4. Let part of the city be fortified by the citizens themselves.

5. Since we have been prevented by the general, we shall not fight.

6. Since the army is being sent into Gaul, there will be danger in Italy.

7. The help of the Romans was most useful to us in that war.

8. Do not be prevented by the words of the enemy.

9. Let not his advice be neglected by our citizens.

10. It is better to send help to our allies than to carry corn to Caesar.

Exercise 134

1. Let the words of the wounded general be heard by all.

2. Let us hear the words of Caesar himself.

3. Since the line has now been drawn up, let us fight bravely.

4. Let all the infantry be hidden in this part of the town.

5. Since the Gauls had now been conquered, he led his men back into camp.

6. Let war be carried on by land and by sea.

7. May the enemy be conquered by the valour of the soldiers, not by stratagem.

8. Since the allies had been placed on the left wing, we were conquered.

9. The king of this nation has sent help to Caesar.

10. It will be more useful to summon a meeting of all the Gauls.

Exercise 135

1. Let two cohorts be sent to Carthage.

2. This thing was quickly announced to the Gauls.

3. Let not the advice of the gods be neglected by men.

4. Since the campaign was being conducted by Caesar, the barbarians were afraid.

5. Let us not be ruled by men whom our fathers conquered.

6. Help will be sent to the allies in three days.

7. Advised by you, he quickly led his men back.

8. May this beautiful city not be seized by the enemy.

9. This nation has always sent help to the Gauls in all the wars.

10. Since the corn has been sent, the hostages will be set free.

SECTION 42

Grammar : **Deponent Verbs.** R.P. pp. 80, 81 :
S.P. pp. 58, 59 : P.G. pp. 146–7.

DEPONENT VERBS

A Deponent Verb is one which is Passive in form but Active in meaning.   But note especially that

(1) It has *all* the Participles (**utens, usurus, usus**), and the Perfect Participle has usually an Active meaning like the rest of the Verb ; e.g. **usus**, *having used.*

(2) The Future Infinitive is of the Active form ; e.g. **usurus esse.**

Exercise 136

1. We encouraged the soldiers with a few words before the battle.

2. We delayed a few days at Athens.

3. The words of our allies encourage us.

4. We do not use arrows in war.

5. We shall encourage our men *when they are* drawn up in line of battle.

6. Our fathers employed the same device.

7. Since there is danger in the city, we shall not delay.

8. *While* exhorting his men he was wounded by an arrow.

9. The leaders of the Gauls are employing our devices.

10. Having exhorted his men with a few words, he will hasten to Carthage.

Exercise 137

1. Having encouraged his men, he drew them up in line of battle.

2. We had never used these shields in war.

3. Let us encourage the defeated soldiers.

4. It is better to stay in the camp than to be conquered.

5. Hindered by the river, they stayed in this land for many days.

6. Let us use our victory well.

7. The gods employ the plans of men.

8. I have never seen the arms which they used.

9. Having delayed a few days in Gaul, they laid waste the fields.

10. Let us employ the help of our allies.

Exericse 138

1. He will not stay many days in Athens.

2. He emboldened the hearts of the soldiers by his valour, not by words.

3. All our plans will be known to the enemy in a few hours.

4. We heard the general encouraging his men.

5. It is better to employ wisdom than courage.

6. Since the enemy had seized the town, we stayed in the fields.

7. This nation does not employ ships in war.

8. It will be most disgraceful now to stay in the camp.

9. The general was about to exhort his soldiers.

10. I have never seen the city in which you are staying.

SECTION 43

Grammar : **Verbs in -*io* of the 3rd Conjugation.**
R.P. p. 84 : S.P. p. 61 : P.G. p. 150.

NOTE.—The Verbs conjugated like **capio** lose the **i** of their
stem **before another i, final e and the syllable ĕr,**

e.g. **cap-it, cape, capĕre.**

Exercise 139

1. They are making a journey through the territories of the
Gauls.

2. Let us take the city which we are attacking.

3. Corn was carried to them on the march by the allies.

4. He does everything by his father's advice.

5. Hasten, soldiers : our city is being taken by the enemy.

6. We captured the ships which the Gauls had sent.

7. The enemy are adopting a bold plan.

8. The Romans were marching to the territories of their
allies.

9. The city, which our fathers saved, will now be taken by
the Gauls.

10. Adopt a bolder plan, Labienus : make an attack on the
enemy.

Exercise 140

1. Let us not delay : let us march against the enemy.

2. Our camp was being taken by the Gauls.

3. Since he has adopted this plan, we shall stay in the camp.

4. It will be more useful to do this than to capture the city.

5. Since the camp was being taken, the soldiers ran into the city.

6. We shall not employ the plan which Caesar adopted.

7. The camp of the Gauls has been taken by our men.

8. The citizens were doing everything that the general had advised.

9. It will be very difficult for us to make a journey through your territories.

10. Since a plan is being formed by the general, we shall summon a meeting.

Exercise 141

1. All will praise the plan you are adopting.

2. Since the city has been very well fortified, let us stay in it.

3. The plan which I had adopted was blamed by all.

4. On the march we saw the forces which our allies had sent.

5. A conquered army will not adopt this plan.

6. The Gauls are now marching through our territories.

7. In a few days they will take the city which we built.

8. The citizens are doing what you advised.

9. Since they are adopting a very bad plan, let us not fear them.

10. *When* preparing war they did the same thing themselves.

SECTION 44

Grammar : **The Verbs** *possum, volo.*   R.P. pp. 85, 88 :
S.P. pp. 62, 65 : P.G. pp. 154, 162–4.

PROLATIVE INFINITIVE

In English Grammar we learn the meaning of an Auxiliary Verb. It is one that is used to help form the tense of another Verb ; e.g. *shall* or *will* in *I shall go, He will go.* The words *I shall, He will* would make no sense unless we either express or understand the Verb which completes them.

There is a large class of Verbs in English which are not thus used to form tenses, but which are like these Auxiliary Verbs in making no complete sense without another Verb following. Such Verbs are *I wish, I intend, I dare, I try, I can, I am able.* The completing Verb which follows them is put in the Infinitive ; e.g. *I wish to speak, He will be able to return.* Sometimes the *to* of the Infinitive is omitted ; e.g. *I can come, I dare say* ; but nevertheless *come* and *say* in these sentences are Infinitives.

The corresponding Verbs in Latin for the most part take the same construction, and the Infinitive following them is called the Prolative Infinitive, but as they do not *all* take the Infinitive only practice can lead to absolute correctness.

Verbs which require another action of the same subject to complete their meaning are usually followed by the Infinitive.

e.g. *We can fight.*
Pugnare possumus.

Notice especially the following as taking this construction in Latin :

(1) Verbs meaning **wish** or **determine** ; e.g. *volo, nolo, malo, constituo.*

(2) Verbs meaning **begin, cease, be accustomed** ; e.g. *incipio, desino, soleo.*

(3) Verbs meaning **be able, dare, ought** ; e.g. *possum, audeo, debeo.*

Exercise 142

1. We wished to do the same ourselves.

2. All were able to see the king *when* exhorting the citizens.

3. The boys could not carry the heavy burden.

4. Warned by his father, he wished to stay in the city.

5. The general cannot send larger forces to the allies.

6. The citizens could not save the city which they loved.

7. We can all fight on behalf of our country.

8. The cavalry will not be able to use their horses.

9. He could not lead his men back before night.

10. We wish to praise the courage of the soldiers.

Exercise 143

1. We could not stay many days in Athens.

2. He cannot set free the hostages, since the Gauls are laying waste our fields.

3. We cannot take the city which we are attacking.

4. They wished to see the general himself.

5. We shall not be able to make a journey through this land.

6. The barbarians had wished to attack our camp.

7. Hindered by the river, they could not withstand our attack.

8. They will not be able to use these weapons in war.

9. The fifth legion could not defeat the cavalry of the Gauls.

10. He is not able to do all that he wishes.

Exercise 144

1. Frightened by Caesar's arrival, the barbarians could not take arms.

2. We are not able to adopt the plan which you advised.

3. We cannot fortify this town with a high rampart.

4. He wishes to conduct the campaign himself.

5. They could not neglect the advice of their own general.

6. He wished to encourage the soldiers before the battle.

7. We all wish to be ruled by the Romans.

8. That part of the city could not be taken by the enemy.

9. Since they could not fight, they stayed in the camp.

10. Since he wished to see the king, he hid himself.

SECTION 45

Grammar : **The Verbs** *nolo, malo.* R.P. p. 88 : S.P. p. 65 :
P.G. pp. 162–4.

The commonest way of expressing a negative command is by
the use of the Imperative of **nolo** followed by the Infinitive.

e.g. *Do not be afraid.*
Noli timere.

Exercise 145

1. We would rather be wounded than conquered.
2. He refused to kill the wounded soldier.
3. He does not wish to march to Rome.
4. They prefer to defeat the enemy by their valour.
5. He was unwilling to be advised by a bad man.
6. They wished to be feared by all men.
7. He prefers to conduct the campaign in our territories.
8. They refused to withstand the enemy's fierce attack.
9. They could not fight more bravely than the enemy.
10. We can adopt a better plan than yours.

Exercise 146

1. We refused to hear the words of the king.

2. They will not be able to stay many days at Carthage.

3. Caesar was unwilling to lead his men back before night.

4. All men would rather be praised than blamed.

5. The boy could not run very quickly, since he had been wounded.

6. Since war is being carried on by land and sea, the danger cannot be avoided.

7. Do not be disturbed by the words of this man.

8. They will be unwilling to attack a Roman legion.

9. We could not see the enemy marching to the city.

10. This state refused to send corn to Caesar.

Exercise 147

1. We cannot withstand so large a number of cavalry.

2. The city could not be fortified in three days.

3. The soldiers would rather be led by you than by me.

4. He was unwilling to stay many days in the same city.

5. Having encouraged the soldiers we summoned a meeting of the citizens.

6. Hidden in the wood they could not see the enemy.

7. Do not praise a man who praises himself.

8. Since he preferred to fight he was sent to the army.

9. It will be very easy to form a safer plan.

10. Do not neglect the words of the god himself.

Section 46

Grammar : **The Verbs *fero, eo.*** R.P. pp. 86, 87 :
S.P. pp. 63, 64 : P.G. pp. 156–161.

Exercise 148

1. We did not wish to go with you [1] to the city.

2. A few soldiers had gone out of the town.

3. He bears everything most bravely.

4. Caesar determined to send help to our allies.

5. We shall go to Rome in five days.

6. Since he had determined to remain, he refused to go.

7. For many days the citizens endured the dangers of war.

8. All good men would rather be conquered than adopt this plan.

9. He went with Caesar to Gaul.

10. Let us go, since the enemy are attacking our allies.

---

[1] The preposition **cum** is placed *after* Personal and Relative Pronouns, the two being written as one word : thus, **mecum, tecum, secum, nobiscum, vobiscum, quocum, quibuscum.**

Exercise 149

1. You will go with me in two hours to the camp.

2. Since they were unwilling to go, we determined to remain.

3. Do not summon a meeting in the city.

4. We saw the general *when he was* going to the war.

5. Having exhorted his soldiers he went to Rome.

6. Since they cannot free their country, they will go to Gaul.

7. The soldiers had endured worse things in war.

8. They are going to the city which they have always wished to see.

9. Let them go : they will not be able to prevent our plan.

10. Since he had not gone with us, he was not captured.

Exercise 150

1. All dangers are borne bravely by good men.

2. The wounded general was borne to the camp.

3. This state had determined to send help to our enemies.

4. It is better to endure danger than to neglect our allies.

5. Since he was going with us, we could not sail.

6. They have decided to kill their king.

7. We cannot endure the praise of this man.

8. Since they have decided to fight, they are going to the camp.

9. Do not place the cavalry on the right wing.

10. I had never seen the town to which we were going.

SECTION 47

Grammar : **The Verb** *fio.* R.P. p. 89 : S.P. p. 66 :
P.G. p. 155.

VERBS REQUIRING A COMPLEMENT

It has been explained (see p. 52) that the Verb *to be* does
not usually make a complete predicate by itself without a Noun
or Adjective for *complement.*

There are other Verbs like this. Without the words in
brackets, the following sentences would make no complete
sense :—He seems (afraid). He is thought (a great man). The
magistrates are named (consuls). He is becoming (wiser).

Intransitive or Passive Verbs meaning (1) *to seem* or *to be
thought,* (2) *to become* or *to be made,* (3) *to be named,* **require a
Complement like the Verb esse,** *to be,* **and this Complement
is always in the same Case as the Subject :**

e.g.   (1) *He seems brave.*
     Fortis videtur.

     Caesar is considered a remarkable man.
     Caesar vir egregius habetur.

  (2) *My brother has been elected consul.*
     Frater meus consul creatus est.

     My son is becoming wiser.
     Filius meus sapientior fit.

  (3) *The magistrates are called consuls.*
     Magistratus consules nominantur.

Exercise 151

1. The boy is now becoming wiser.

2. Since he had never been conquered, he was considered a remarkable man.

3. He seems a bolder man than his brother.

4. Their camp seemed smaller than ours.

5. The captives seemed very wretched.

6. We wish to be guided by the advice of the wise.

7. This city seemed to us most beautiful.

8. We did not wish to become allies of this nation.

9. May you become wiser than your father.

10. All praised the remarkable valour of the tenth legion.

Exercise 152

1. The customs of our fathers seem to have been very good.

2. You cannot become wiser than your brother.

3. He would rather be considered brave than good.

4. Having been made general, he advised us very well.

5. Nothing can hinder the enemy *when* marching against us.

6. He seems a better man than his father.

7. Since he could not become general, he remained at Rome.

8. Their territories seem broader than ours.

9. He seems to have determined to go with us.

10. Since he had fought well in Gaul, he was considered useful to the state.

Exercise 153

1. The gods seem to have prevented our plans.

2. The ships seemed very large to the barbarians.

3. Since he could not be general, he preferred to remain at Carthage.

4. They seem to use these weapons in all their battles.

5. You are considered by all the bravest general.

6. Having stayed a few years in Athens, he became a wiser man.

7. Since he has conquered the Gauls, he is considered a great man.

8. He who neglects the advice of wise men never becomes wise himself.

9. Since he was considered useful to the state, he was not condemned.

10. Your father was considered very wise by all the citizens.

SECTION 48

When the Verbs described in the last rule are Transitive and used in the Active Voice, the Complement is in agreement with the Object ;

e.g.   *The people made him consul.*
Populus eum consulem creavit.

They call the magistrate a consul.
Magistratum consulem nominant.

They thought him a distinguished man.
Hunc egregium virum putabant.

Exercise 154

1. This year the people will elect Cotta consul.

2. In that city the magistrates are not elected by the people.

3. Those who free their country I call good men.

4. Since he was considered useful to the state, they elected him consul.

5. We cannot call a general who has been conquered, successful.

6. I would rather be a consul of the Roman people than the leader of an army.

7. Since he has always advised us well, we call him wise.

8. The people will not elect you magistrate.

9. He is called wise by all who have seen him.

10. Since he had been elected consul, he decided to go to the city.

Exercise 155

1. The Roman citizens were unwilling to call Caesar king.

2. He seemed wiser than his father.

3. Having been condemned by the magistrate, he could not remain at Rome.

4. He wishes to be elected consul by the citizens.

5. The Roman people has decided to name you general.

6. The citizens dare not elect him consul.

7. Since we have appointed Caesar general, the state will be safe.

8. Since he had endured many dangers, he was thought a brave man.

9. We cannot condemn a man whom the Roman people has appointed magistrate.

10. Let them not dare to call me base.

Exercise 156

1. Since he endures everything on behalf of his country, we call him a good man.

2. We dared not send corn to the Roman army.

3. Since he could do everything, he seemed a remarkable man.

4. He has never dared to summon a meeting of citizens.

5. Since he refused to be elected consul, he was praised by all.

6. Terrified by their shouts, he ran to the magistrates.

7. Since we were hindered by the river, we dared not go.

8. Since he seemed useful to the state, he was elected consul.

9. The prisoners whom we condemned will be set free by the magistrate.

10. The enemy dared not attack a Roman legion.

SECTION 49

Grammar : **Interrogative Pronoun.**
R.P. p. 51 : S.P. p. 32 : P.G. p. 104.

QUESTIONS

I. Questions can be asked in Latin as in English by **Interrogative Pronouns or Adverbs.**

e.g.   *Who is he ?*
          Quis est ?
          Why are you afraid ?
          Cur times ?

II. When there is no such word English makes the question clear by the order of the words, e.g. *Is he a friend ?* But Latin has no such fixed order, and either *amicus est* or. *est amicus* could mean *He is a friend.* Therefore it uses **Interrogative Particles** which mark the sentence as a question but do not need to be translated by a separate word in English The usual ones are

(1) **-ne,** which has to be appended to a principal word ;

e.g.   *Is he a friend ?*
          Amicusne est ?

When the sentence has the negative *non* the -*ne* is appended to this word, making **nonne.** A sentence in this form shows that the answer *yes* is expected ;

e.g.   *Is he not a friend ?*
          Nonne amicus est ?

(2) **num,** which puts the question in such a way that the answer *no* is expected ;

> e.g.   *Is he (really) a friend ?*
> **Num amicus est ?**

Exercise 157

1. Who has dared to adopt this plan ?

2. What shall we be able to do at Rome ?

3. Why did they set free the hostages which we sent ?

4. Who will be elected consul this year ?

5. What did you see in that part of the city ?

6. Why was this cohort led back into the camp ?

7. Who is unwilling to endure dangers on behalf of his country ?

8. Why were consuls not elected that year at Rome ?

9. By whom have the fields of our allies been laid waste ?

10. To whom did your leader announce this victory ?

Exercise 158

1. What are you doing? The city is being taken by the enemy.

2. Why did you place the cavalry on the right wing?

3. Did you not see the Roman soldiers building ships?

4. Do you really consider our general a brave man?

5. Have you done what your father advised?

6. Did not the general exhort his soldiers?

7. You will always be considered the friend of the Roman people.

8. Cannot this nation send corn to our army?

9. Does he really wish to set free the men whom we condemned?

10. Shall you stay many days at Rome?

Exercise 159

1. Is it really useful to the state to have a large number of ships?

2. Is not praise welcome to all men?

3. Have they really dared to attack a Roman legion?

4. Will the cries of the citizens be heard by the king?

5. Will you really adopt a plan which is blamed by all?

6. Did you not hear the words of your father?

7. Why have you neglected the advice of the wisest men?

8. Who will be willing to remain at Carthage?

9. What did you send to your father?

10. Why are the men whom we conquered fighting again?

SECTION 50

Grammar : **Apposition and Composite Subject.**
R.P. pp. 117, 118 : S.P. p. 76.

APPOSITION

A Noun, added directly to another Noun in order to describe it further, is said to be in Apposition with it.

A Noun in Apposition with another Noun agrees with it in Case ;

e.g. *Caesar, a very brave man, conquered the Gauls.*
Caesar, vir fortissimus, Gallos vicit.

I have often seen Caesar, our great general.
Saepe Caesarem vidi, magnum nostrum imperatorem.

We have the Roman legions, a great protection.
Legiones Romanas habemus, magnum praesidium.

Notice especially

The city of Rome.
Urbs Roma.

The town of Verona.
Oppidum Verona.

In such expressions Latin puts the name in Apposition " the city Rome," " the town Vérona," and does not say " the city *of* Rome," etc.

COMPOSITE SUBJECT

If a Verb has more than one Subject the rules for **Number** and **Person** will be the same as in English, viz. :—

(1) The Verb will be in the Plural.

(2) If the Subjects differ in Person the Verb will be in the 1st rather than in the 2nd, and in the 2nd rather than in the 3rd.

> e.g.   *Both my son and I shall come.*[1]
> **Et ego et filius meus veniemus.**

Note the order of the Latin in this sentence. The *First Person* Subject comes first in Latin, last in English.

The rule for the **Gender** of a Participle or Adjective Complement when there are two Subjects is as follows :—

(1) If the Subjects are of the same Gender the Participle or Adjective agrees with them.

(2) If the Subjects differ in Gender—

> (*a*) When the Subjects are *persons* the Participle or Adjective is in the Masculine rather than the Feminine.

> e.g.   *Both my father and mother remained at Rome.*
> **Et pater meus et mater Romae morati sunt.**

> (*b*) When the Subjects are *lifeless things* it is most usual to make both Verb and Complement agree with the nearest Subject only, but often the Complement is put in the Neuter Plural. As this rule is difficult, no instances will occur in the present exercises.

---

[1] Do not confuse with these those sentences in which the Subjects are connected by [*Either*] . . . *or* . . . ; e.g. [*Either*] *my brother or my sister is coming.* This is not a double Subject—the two Subjects are alternative—and in Latin as in English the Verb will then agree with the *nearest* Subject.

ADJECTIVES AGREEING WITH TWO NOUNS

If an Adjective qualifies *as an Attribute* more than one Noun, make it agree with the nearest ; e.g.

He maintained his kingship by his great influence and wealth.

Magna et auctoritate et opibus regnum obtinebat.

Exercise 160

1. You and I will go with the army to Gaul.

2. The city of Rome was taken by the Gauls.

3. Caesar, the consul, will come to our city.

4. You will have the Roman legions, a great protection.

5. You and your son were blamed by all the citizens.

6. Rome, the largest city of Italy, will be taken by the enemy.

7. You and I cannot bear aid to the wounded soldiers.

8. Will they not go to the city of Athens ?

9. Who can withstand the fierce attack of our troops ?

10. By his great wisdom and wealth he will maintain his kingship for many years.

Exercise 161

1. You and he were unwilling to come with us.

2. What will Cotta, a Roman citizen, be able to do on behalf of us ?

3. His father and mother dared not stay in Rome.

4. The town of Verona is being attacked by the Gauls.

5. He and I were coming from Athens to Rome.

6. Cotta and I will bear aid to the conquered allies.

7. Why did you not consider me a friend of the Roman people ?

8. Shall you really use all the weapons which you are carrying ?

9. You and your friend have neglected the advice of your father.

10. Since he had come to us, we dared not go with you.

Exercise 162

1. Did you see your friend coming to the city ?

2. Since you and I have been condemned, we shall be killed.

3. Having stayed three days in the town of Verona, he came to us.

4. You and Caesar have carried on many wars.

5. His son had obtained the kingship by his great valour and wealth.

6. Your father and mother have dared to set free a condemned prisoner.

7. Having been elected consul, he exhorted the citizens with a few words.

8. Has this state really dared to send corn to the town of Verona ?

9. You and I will call a meeting of all the citizens.

10. Why have you, a Roman consul, come against us who are considered your allies ?

SECTION 51

Grammar : **Accusative and Genitive Cases.**
R.P. pp. 120–122, 133–139 : S.P. pp. 77, 82–84.

---

(1) Double Accusative.—Some Verbs of *teaching* (especially **doceo**) and *asking* may take two Accusatives, one of the person, the other of the thing ;

> e.g.   *He taught me letters.*
> **Litteras me docuit.**
>
> *I ask you your opinion.*
> **Rogo te sententiam.**[1]

(2) Partitive Genitive.—Any word that signifies a *part* can be followed by a Genitive signifying that of which it is a part.

This is called the Partitive Genitive. In English we express it by the Preposition *of* ;

> e.g.   *A portion of the Britons.*
> **Pars Britannorum.**
>
> *The bravest of the Britons.*
> **Fortissimi Britannorum.**

---

[1] Except in the phrase *rogare sententiam* use *rogo* with two Accusatives only when the second object is a Neuter Pronoun. With a Neuter Pronoun for one object the Verb *celo* (conceal) can also take two Accusatives ;

> e.g   *I hide this from Caesar.*
> **Hoc Caesarem celo.**

Exercise 163

1. Having been elected magistrate, he asked me my opinion.

2. Since he wished to stay in the city, he went to the consul.

3. Let us teach them everything ourselves.

4. Why did you not ask your father his opinion ?

5. Who sent so great a number of cavalry to the town of Verona ?

6. Did not your father, the wisest of all men, teach you this ?

7. *When he was* going to the city I asked him his opinion.

8. Do not come with us : it will be safer to remain at Rome.

9. The Britons used these weapons in all battles.

10. For five days the hostages which we had sent were detained in the camp.

Exercise 164

1. The general whose army conquered us has been elected consul.

2. Having been sent to Rome, he announced the victory to the magistrate.

3. You will not be able to teach me many things : I have been taught by my father.

4. The boldest of the soldiers were terrified by the arrival of the general himself.

5. It is easier to teach boys letters than to conduct a campaign.

6. Are not the bravest of the Gauls fighting against our legions ?

7. War has been waged for many years against the Britons.

8. This was the most difficult route of all.

9. Since I have been elected consul, I shall not be able to go with you.

10. We have borne aid to the Romans *when* conquered.

Exercise 165

1. They were going from Rome to the city in which were the captives.

2. You and I will teach the boy letters.

3. The greatest part of this city has been fortified with a high rampart.

4. It is better to have conquered the enemy than to have taught boys letters.

5. Were not wounded men borne to the camp by us ?

6. The bravest of the soldiers refused to use shields.

7. For many years he held the kingship of the Britons.

8. My father and mother were killed by this king.

9. The citizens did not dare to elect this man magistrate.

10. Do not blame the general : he could not hold that part of the town.

SECTION 52

Grammar : **Dative Case.**   R.P. pp. 123–127 :
S.P. pp. 78, 79.

---

(1) The Dative after Intransitive Verbs.

The Dative of the Indirect Object following a Transitive
Verb has been explained on page 14.

An **Intransitive Verb,** though it has no Direct Object, can
take an Indirect Object, whenever its sense permits ;

> e.g.   *To be subject to kings.*
> **Servire regibus.**
>
> *To yield to the enemy.*
> **Hosti cedere.**

**Many of the commonest of these Intransitive Verbs cor-
respond to Verbs that are Transitive in English ;**

> e.g.   *To obey*   **parere** (=*to be obedient to*).

Those required in the following exercises are given in the
vocabulary.

(2) The Dative of the Possessor.

A Dative can be used with the Verb *esse* to express the
Possessor ;

> e.g.   *I have three brothers.*
> **Sunt mihi tres fratres**
> (literally, *There are to me three brothers*).

Exercise 166

1. The allies were unwilling to obey our general.

2. A small number of the Gauls was at that time subject to the Romans.

3. Did not my mother teach your sister letters ?

4. Since you and I have obeyed the consul, we shall be set free.

5. Between the camp and the river was the town of Verona.

6. It will be better to obey our leader than to seize a kingdom.

7. Your brother and sister dared not come to Rome.

8. Let us yield to the advice of those who are exhorting us.

9. This boy has a brother and a sister.

10. Is it not better to be subject to the Romans than to do this ?

Exercise 167

1. Having been elected magistrate, he refused to obey his father.

2. Who will bear aid to the wounded soldiers ?

3. By his remarkable valour he defeated the boldest nation of all Gaul.

4. Do not yield to an enemy whom our fathers conquered.

5. Since they were subject to us, they could not bear aid to the Gauls.

6. You and I cannot use the weapons which the Britons use.

7. War was being waged between the Romans and Gauls.

8. Is your brother really considered very wise ?

9. Since he obeys his father, he is considered a good boy.

10. These men to whom you wish to yield, have often been conquered.

Exercise 168

1. Let us not yield to a conquered enemy.

2. Did you see him taking arms to the camp?

3. The king does not use his wealth well.

4. The citizens of this state were subject to the Romans.

5. Those who obey the gods we consider the friends of their country.

6. We, who have conducted many campaigns, will not yield to you.

7. The worst of the citizens wished to be subject to kings.

8. What shall you do at Rome? Shall you be able to see the consul?

9. He has a brother who will be elected consul.

10. Between your country and ours there is broad sea.

SECTION 53

Grammar : **Ablative Case.** R.P. pp. 128–132 :
S.P. pp. 80–82.

---

(1) We have had (page 14) the Ablative used to express
the *instrument.* It can also be used to express the **cause.**

e.g. *He perished of hunger.*
Fame periit.

(2) A few Deponent Verbs take an Ablative where the corresponding English has a Direct Object. The commonest are
utor and **potior.**

e.g. *Let us use these books.*
His libris utamur.
He obtains (possession of) the kingdom.
Regno potitur.

Exercise 169

1. His father holds the kingship which he obtained through his wealth.

2. The citizens whom we conquered are perishing of hunger.

3. Let us use the book which your father sent.

4. Do not ask me my opinion.

5. Who can rule a people well without wisdom ?

6. Those who now obey us will not dare to fight.

7. Let us teach our sons to use weapons.

8. It is better to perish of hunger than to be subject to a king.

9. You and I will return to the city in a few days.

10. Who would rather stay at Carthage than see Italy ?

Exercise 170

1. Let us return to the town through these fields.

2. You will not be able to conquer the barbarians without the help of the allies.

3. Having stayed ten days at Rome, they are now returning to Gaul.

4. We shall take the city and obtain possession of the kingdom.

5. It is more disgraceful to yield than to be conquered.

6. He could not teach his brother without his father's help.

7. Did you see the army returning to the camp ?

8. They will come in a few days and set free the prisoners.

9. Take this book : use it well.

10. The boldest of the soldiers would rather perish than yield.

Exercise 171

1. Why are the citizens perishing of hunger? Let us summon a meeting.

2. The king whom we obey is considered the worst of all men.

3. You and your father will return on the tenth day.

4. The fifth legion was returning with him to the camp.

5. We dared not return to the father without his son.

6. This nation had never yielded to a Roman army.

7. They have obtained possession of the city which they were attacking.

8. It is not disgraceful to obey a magistrate whom we ourselves elected.

9. He always seemed to himself the wisest of men.

10. Since the cohort has not returned, we shall perish of hunger.

Section 54

Grammar : **Parts of Verbs.** R.P. pp. 98, 99 :
S.P. p. 69 : P.G. pp. 170–2.

Exercise 172

1. The book which you sent I gave to my sister.

2. Do not help the men who have destroyed our city.

3. Since he had stood under the wall for three hours, he saw everything.

4. May the number of soldiers and ships be increased !

5. Give me the book : you cannot use it.

6. The forces which you sent have been destroyed by the enemy.

7. We have increased the number of our ships this year.

8. Who gave you the books that you use now ?

9. Did you help your brother with your advice ?

10. Has that part of the city been destroyed ?

Exercise 173

1. Did not the barbarians fight very fiercely ?
2. You and I have given advice to Caesar.
3. Has not your brother conducted the campaign very well ?
4. Do not bear aid to men who obey the Romans.
5. Do you not think him a very wise man ?
6. What did you give to the soldier who announced the victory ?
7. The gods help those who dare everything.
8. What I have not seen I cannot praise.
9. He would rather be conquered than increase the number of ships.
10. Help us, Romans : our citizens are perishing of hunger.

Exercise 174

1. The men to whom you gave this advice are returning.
2. Since he had destroyed the citizens, he obtained the sovereignty.
3. Cotta, the leader of the Roman army, will come in a few days.
4. Since their city had been destroyed, they could not help us.
5. On the march we were attacked by large forces of Gauls.
6. Having encouraged the soldiers, he returned to the city.
7. Nothing is more pleasant than to help our friends.
8. What you have taught me will be most useful.
9. The number of Roman citizens has now been increased.
10. We gave corn to the soldiers who were perishing of hunger.

SECTION 55

Grammar : **Parts of Verbs.** R.P. pp. 100–102 :
S.P. p. 70 : P.G. pp. 172–6, 185–6.

Exercise 175

1. The soldiers who had come with Labienus told us this.

2. Caesar has departed with all his army.

3. They have not received the corn which you sent.

4. Since they have told us nothing, let us go to the consul.

5. We ascertained this from spies which we sent into the fields.

6. We shall not retreat into a city which is held by the Romans.

7. Have you received the hostages which we sent ?

8. Let us join our forces with the army of Labienus.

9. You and I will depart to Italy.

10. This was ascertained through spies sent by Caesar.

Exercise 176

1. Do not retreat into our country : we are friends of the Roman people.

2. We have ascertained much about the Gauls through spies.

3. Since he had conducted many campaigns successfully, he was unwilling to retreat.

4. They retreated into the city, which they had freed from the enemy.

5. Caesar had not received hostages from this state.

6. The Romans who were attacking us have departed.

7. Labienus held this place with a small garrison.

8. Since they had given us corn, we were unwilling to destroy their city.

9. Who told your father this ? Did he blame you ?

10. From this place we marched to the sea.

Exercise 177

1. You and I will retreat to this place.

2. We were returning to this place by the same route.

3. Having stayed many days in Rome, he wished to depart.

4. We announced the victory to him *when he was* retreating into the camp.

5. Since they are adopting this plan, let us depart.

6. You and I will be able to hold this place with a small garrison.

7. They have given much to the citizens, who are perishing of hunger.

8. Since the allies have not come, Caesar has moved his camp.

9. We cannot accept advice from the man who destroyed the city.

10. Let us retreat to the river, which is between the city and the camp.

SECTION 56

Grammar : **Parts of Verbs.** R.P. pp. 103, 104 :
S.P. p. 71 ; P.G. pp. 177–182.

Exercise 178

1. We will spare the citizens, since they have given us corn.

2. We routed the enemy whom we had attacked.

3. Do not fly to the camp : the allies are coming.

4. Let us leave the captives in the city.

5. The citizens defended the town which the Gauls attacked.

6. All kinds of weapons were known to the Roman soldiers.

7. It was the custom of the Romans to spare a conquered enemy.

8. They have routed the army which we sent.

9. These places are known to us through spies.

10. We believe the allies who have always helped us.

Exercise 179

1. Have not the forces which we sent been routed ?
2. Do not return to the city from which you have departed.
3. Why are they flying ? The camp has not been taken.
4. You and I have always spared the conquered.
5. This was ascertained by the general through spies.
6. He believed me : why does he not believe you ?
7. The captives who were left in the city seem very wretched.
8. We received the flying soldiers into the camp.
9. They cannot defend the town which we are attacking.
10. Since the general had returned, we dared not fly.

Exercise 180

1. Let us return before night : it is a very difficult journey.
2. They have left their heaviest weapons in the camp.
3. Since he had come from the consul, we believed him.
4. These places are known to the enemy whom we are attacking.
5. Since we could hear the general's voice, we dared not fly.
6. Caesar will move his camp before the fifth hour of the day.
7. The city has been taken : the enemy are flying.
8. Having been left in the city, he could not bear arms.
9. It is disgraceful not to spare a flying enemy.
10. Since you say this, we are willing to return.

SECTION 57

Grammar : **Parts of Verbs.** R.P. pp. 105, 106 :
S.P. p. 72 : P.G. pp. 183, 187.

Exercise 181

1. The enemy were following the Roman army.

2. We shall start in a few hours.

3. Having followed up our column for several days, they returned to their city.

4. Having set out with him, we could not leave him.

5. The Romans were praised by all on account of their courage.

6. It is better to die than to be taken by the enemy.

7. Men are dying of hunger in this city.

8. The enemy are following by an easier route.

9. Do not tell them this : they know it already.

10. On the march we saw their cavalry returning.

Exercise 182

1. Many things were done by the citizens on that day.

2. His brother and sister died at Rome.

3. Several of the soldiers were left in the camp.

4. You and I will start in three days for Rome.

5. The legion which was sent to us has departed.

6. After the battle Caesar moved his camp.

7. Having followed for several days, we came to a river.

8. The army has set out with the general whom we appointed.

9. The Gauls will follow our column for several days.

10. Since he has been wounded by an arrow, he will die in a few hours.

Exercise 183

1. Having been left in the town, the prisoners died of hunger.

2. Our men made an attack on the enemy *when they were* retreating.

3. Nothing can be more base than to wound a dying man.

4. We shall not spare the soldiers who are following us.

5. You and your brother did not follow the flying enemy.

6. Do you really believe the man who said this ?

7. We drove several of the Gauls into their camp.

8. Do not we Romans always spare a conquered enemy ?

9. It will be very easy to pursue them *when they are* retreating.

10. We shall follow the soldiers who are now setting out.

SECTION 58

Grammar : **Gender of Nouns. 1st and 2nd Declensions, and 3rd Declension (Masculine Terminations with exceptions).** See Rules on pp. 156–157.[1]

Exercise 184

1. The Roman sailors refused to leave their ships.

2. By this talk the fear of the citizens was increased.

3. There were many trees and most beautiful flowers in this place.

4. We saw the bones of the soldiers who had been killed in that war.

5. The bold faces of the enemy terrified our men.

6. These boats are smaller than (those) of the Gauls.

7. You will not dare to pursue so great a multitude.

8. Let us make an attack on the confused ranks of the Romans.

9. Rest was given to the soldiers by the general.

10. Caesar encouraged the soldiers by this speech.

---

[1] From this point the Gender of the Nouns required in the Exercises will not be given in the Special Vocabularies.

Exercise 185

1. The soldiers will receive this reward from the state.

2. Many boats were following our ships.

3. The horse's foot had been wounded by an arrow.

4. Your conversation had been heard by the general.

5. Rest was welcome to the soldiers who had started at night.

6. After this speech they were unwilling to spare him.

7. His face had been wounded by a dart.

8. A reward has been given to the men who defended the town.

9. These sailors gave us a few boats.

10. Did you not see this tree and these flowers ?

Exercise 186

1. To whom did you give the reward ?

2. Do not follow this multitude of citizens.

3. This tree was left in the field by my father.

4. The confused ranks of the enemy could not withstand our attack.

5. My speech was heard very easily by everybody.

6. Let us not give them a reward which they will not dare to accept.

7. By much labour we can all obtain wealth.

8. We could not see the faces of the sailors.

9. What did you say to the man who has increased our work ?

10. All who heard your speech praised it.

SECTION 59

Grammar : **Gender of Nouns. 3rd Declension (Feminine Terminations with exceptions).**
See Rules on pp. 156–158.

Exercise 187

1. That summer we sustained a great disaster in Italy.

2. We dared not neglect your safety.

3. A few boats were following our fleet.

4. This mountain had been seized by our infantry.

5. This law has always been neglected in our state.

6. We shall lead a large army into your boundaries.

7. This winter many will die of hunger in the city.

8. Having followed our fleet for three days, they sailed to Athens.

9. In this valley there are very many trees and most beautiful flowers.

10. The bridge was made by the soldiers with much labour.

Exercise 188

1. Let us not accept this peace, citizens.
2. There are many flocks in this valley.
3. Who will dare to announce this disaster to the king ?
4. Do not neglect our safety : we are dying of hunger.
5. By this fraud he has obtained much wealth.
6. Our army has sustained a great disaster : let us defend the city.
7. Having started that summer from Rome, he marched into our boundaries.
8. This reward was given to those who had saved our fleet.
9. Your flocks were praised by all who had seen them.
10. On this hill we saw the enemy's line drawn up.

Exercise 189

1. That winter the citizens were perishing of hunger.
2. By this peace the city was saved.
3. We dared not depart from the mountain near which we had pitched the camp.
4. By this fraud he obtained a large reward.
5. Since we have sustained this disaster, let us not return to Rome.
6. Having set out from the camp, we came to this mountain.
7. On this hill there are many trees, beneath which we shall be able to hide ourselves.
8. These laws will be most useful to our state.
9. It will be very easy to obtain wealth by this fraud.
10. This mountain had been seized by the soldiers whom we had sent.

SECTION 60

Grammar : **Gender of Nouns.** **3rd Declension (Neuter Terminations with exceptions), 4th and 5th Declensions.** See Rules on pp. 156–158.

Exercise 190

1. We did not see many animals in this land.

2. These nets will be most useful to the sailors.

3. We have determined to leave a small fleet in this harbour.

4. Your poem will be praised by all your friends.

5. The knees of these animals are very small.

6. A small band of soldiers set out for this hill.

7. Your name is feared by the enemies of our state.

8. The flashes of lightning terrified the barbarians with whom we were fighting.

9. These spurs were left in the camp by the cavalry.

10. We received corn and milk from these barbarians.

Exercise 191

1. Let us not leave on the ships the bodies of men who died for their country.

2. This house was built by the Romans who conquered our fathers.

3. His head was wounded by an arrow.

4. Beneath this oak stands the house in which you taught me letters.

5. In these woods we saw many animals.

6. From whom did you ascertain the general's name ?

7. In this valley stood a little house and a few trees.

8. Caesar determined to seize this mountain before night.

9. A little band of Romans was fighting against a large multitude of Gauls.

10. We decided to pitch our camp between the river and this hill.

Exercise 192

1. Did not a small band of our men rout a large multitude of the enemy ?

2. This house stands near the mountain to which we are coming.

3. This reward was given to the consul who defended our city.

4. We have conquered the enemy : the ships are returning to the harbour.

5. Beneath this hill there is a valley in which we saw many flowers and trees.

6. His face is known to me : his name I could not ascertain.

7. These animals have small feet, large heads.

8. Having been routed by the enemy, they dared not return to Rome.

9. Caesar dared not pitch his camp in this valley.

10. That harbour will not take many ships.

GENDER SHOWN BY MEANING

Gender is properly the Grammatical distinction that indicates sex.   Therefore

(1) A Noun that stands for a male or a nation is **Masculine** : e.g. consul, *a consul* ; Persae, *Persians*.

(2) A Noun that stands for a female is **Feminine,** e.g. mulier, *a woman*.

(3) Many Nouns can stand for male or female persons or animals. These are called **Common** in Gender, and they can be Masculine or Feminine according to the sense : e.g. civis, *citizen* ; testis, *witness* ; sacerdos, *priest* or *priestess* ; canis, *dog*.

In English the names of *things*, which cannot be male or female, are all called **Neuter,** and this is a natural distinction. But this does not hold in Latin.   The names of things that have no natural Gender may in Latin be Masculine, Feminine, or Neuter, and their Genders must be learnt by practice.

But as particular *terminations* in the different Declensions for the most part belong to particular Genders, it is possible to lay down certain rules. The following are the most important ones with the commonest exceptions. There are many other exceptions in less common Nouns.

GENDER AS SHOWN BY TERMINATION

DECLENSION I

RULES.	EXCEPTIONS.
-A Fem.	Masc. are some denoting males; e.g. **nauta,** *sailor,* **poeta,** *poet.*
-AS, -ES Masc.	

DECLENSION II

RULES.	EXCEPTION.
-US, -ER Masc.	Fem. **humus.**
-UM Neut.	

DECLENSION III

RULES.   EXCEPTIONS.

(*a*) Masculine in

-O	Fem. in **-io, -go,** and **-do** (*except* **ordo**).
-OR	Fem. **arbor.** Neut. **cor.**
-OS	— Neut. **ōs, ŏs.**
-ER	Fem. **linter.** Neut. **iter, ver.**
-ES (with Genitive increasing)	Fem. **merces, quies.**

RULES.	EXCEPTIONS.
(b) Feminine in	
-IS	Besides many that are Common from their meaning (e.g. **civis**, *citizen*), the following are regularly Masculine : **amnis, cinis, collis, crinis, ensis, finis, ignis, lapis, mensis, orbis, panis, piscis, pulvis, sanguis.**
-AS	—
-AUS	—
-ES (Genitive not increasing)	—
-ŬS	— Neut. **crus, ius, rus.**
-X	Masc. all in **-ex**, except **lex.**
-S preceded by a consonant	Masc. **dens, fons, mons, pons.**
(c) Neuter in	
-AR	
-UR	Masc. **fur.**
-ŬS	Fem. **pecŭs (pecudis).**
-L, -A, -N, -C, -E, -T	Masc. **sol, consul.**

DECLENSION IV

RULES.	EXCEPTIONS.
-US Masc.	Fem. are names of **trees** and **domus, tribus, manus.**
-U Neut.	

DECLENSION V

RULE.	EXCEPTION.
-ES Fem.	Masc. is **dies** in its ordinary sense of *day*. It can be Fem. in the sense of *time* or *date*.

LATIN-ENGLISH EXERCISES

LATIN-ENGLISH EXERCISES

I. (Ex. 1–3)

1. Amabit.
2. Laborat.
3. Amant.
4. Maturabo.
5. Pugnabimus.

6. Maturat.
7. Amabunt.
8. Maturabit.
9. Pugnabis.
10. Laboras.

II. (Ex. 4–6)

1. Errabit.
2. Amavit.
3. Pugnavimus.
4. Laboravi.
5. Erraverunt.

6. Pugnabunt.
7. Maturavisti.
8. Erravisti.
9. Maturavimus.
10. Amavistis.

III. (Ex. 7–9)

1. Maturabat.
2. Laboravi.
3. Pugnabant.
4. Maturavit.
5. Errabam.

6. Amabamus.
7. Maturabitis.
8. Errabamus.
9. Laboraverunt.
10. Pugnabatis.

IV. (Ex. 10–12)

1. Pugnaverat.
2. Maturaveramus.
3. Maturavimus.
4. Navigabit.
5. Laboravit.

6. Laboraverat.
7. Pugnaveram.
8. Navigaveras.
9. Maturavistis.
10. Pugnaveratis.

V. (Ex. 13–15)

1. Maturaverimus.
2. Maturaveramus.
3. Erraveris.
4. Navigavit.
5. Navigaverit.

6. Pugnavi.
7. Erravisti.
8. Navigaveramus.
9. Pugnavimus.
10. Pugnaverimus.

VI. (Ex. 16–18)

1. Belgas oppugnavero.
2. Belgae copias oppugnaverunt.
3. Belgae patriam amabunt.
4. Pugnam nuntiaveratis.
5. Cotta victoriam nuntiaverit.

6. Belgae pugnam nuntiabant.
7. Maturabat Cotta.
8. Cotta Belgas oppugnat.
9. Patriam Belgae amant.
10. Belgae Cottam oppugnaverint.

VII.   (Ex. 19-21)

1. Belgarum copias oppugnabis.
2. Belgae victoriam amabant.
3. Belgarum copias oppugnaveramus.
4. Belgae Cottam sagitta vulneraverunt.
5. Belgarum copias oppugnaverat.
6. Belgas sagittis vulneraverant.
7. Belgarum victoriam nuntiabit.
8. Victoriam Belgis nuntiavit.
9. Belgae patriam sapientia servaverunt.
10. Victoriam Belgis nuntiabimus.

VIII.   (Ex. 22-24)

1. Barbari patriam amant.
2. Barbari Marcum non amant.
3. Labienum sagitta vulneraverant.
4. Labienus barbaros non amat.
5. Romani Labienum amaverunt.
6. Romani et barbari pugnabunt.
7. Romani barbaros superaverint.
8. Barbarorum equos sagittis vulnerant.
9. Romani barbaros superant.
10. Romanorum victoriam nuntiabunt.

IX. (Ex. 25-27)

1. Barbari periculum vitabunt.
2. Romanos telis vulnerabunt.
3. Barbaros consilio superavimus.
4. Romani bellum parabant.
5. Equum telo vulneravisti.
6. Oppidum Labienus oppugnavit.
7. Castra consilio servavit.
8. Romani consilio barbaros superabunt.
9. Castra barbari oppugnaverunt.
10. Bellum parabant barbari.

X. (Ex. 28-30)

1. Puerum telo vulneravisti.
2. Barbarorum tela pueri vitabant.
3. Agros Gallorum vastaveratis.
4. Pueri equum sagitta vulneraverat.
5. Agros Romanorum Galli vastabant.
6. Galli belli pericula vitabunt.
7. Gallos, Labiene, non superabis.
8. Nostri oppida Gallorum oppugnaverant.
9. Labienum pueri amabant.
10. Pueri patriam amant.

XI. (Ex. 31–33)

1. Pueros parvos magna pericula terrent.
2. Magna pericula pueri timent.
3. Non magnam sapientiam Belgae habebant.
4. Pueri bonos equos amant.
5. Magna belli pericula, Labiene, vitaveris.
6. Boni pugnas non amant.
7. Pueri parvi errabant.
8. Nostri magnas sagittas non habuerunt.
9. Belli pericula timeo.
10. Parva oppida Galli habebant.

XII. (Ex. 34–36)

1. Miseros captivos terruerunt.
2. Magna pericula non timuerit.
3. Pueros miseros barbari terrent.
4. Miserorum Gallorum agros vastabat.
5. Nostri barbaros terruerant.
6. Galli pulchra oppida habebant.
7. Nostri scuta magna habebant.
8. Belgae nostros sagittis terruerant.
9. Equi Gallorum tela timebant.
10. Miseri pueri laborant.

XIII. (Ex. 37–39)

1. Labienus Romanorum copias ducebat.
2. Multas et pulchras terras reges.
3. Cottae consilia neglexit.
4. Multa belli pericula vitavit.
5. Arma non habebant miseri captivi.
6. Bonorum consilia non neglegit.
7. Parvas copias barbarorum ducet.
8. Pueri parvi arma non habent.
9. Magna pericula magna sapientia superavit.
10. Multa Gallorum oppida vastaverat.

XIV. (Ex. 40–42)

1. Copias Romanas in castra imperator duxerat.
2. Milites Romanos in oppidum duxerit.
3. Romanorum victoriam imperatori nuntiaverunt.
4. Milites Romani arma parabant.
5. Patriam bonis consiliis rexerit.
6. Imperatoris victoriam militibus nuntiabimus.
7. Equites Romani barbaros superaverunt.
8. Imperatoris consilium non neglexerat.
9. Equites in castra ducent.
10. Dux consilio milites servavit.

XV. (Ex. 43-45)

1. Imperator militum clamores audivit.
2. Romani oppidum aggere muniunt.
3. Civium magnos clamores audiet.
4. Labienus equites contra aggerem duxit.
5. Belgae castra aggeribus muniebant.
6. Civium miserorum clamores Romani audiverunt.
7. Hostium castra telis oppugnavimus.
8. Miseri pueri barbarorum clamores audiverunt.
9. Hostes oppida aggeribus muniverunt.
10. Barbarorum duces castra Romana oppugnabunt.

XVI. (Ex. 46-48)

1. Barbarorum ingentes copias non timebimus.
2. Galli omnia oppida muniverant.
3. Omnes hostium clamores audiverant.
4. Oppida omnia aggeribus muniverint.
5. Galli oppidum ingenti aggere muniverunt.
6. Miserorum civium clamores audiveris.
7. Equites ingentes copias Gallorum oppugnabunt.
8. Magnos militum clamores audiveras.
9. Imperator omnes copias in urbem ducet.
10. Omnes barbari ingentia arma habebant.

XVII. (Ex. 49–51)

1. Imperator a militibus Romanis amatur.
2. Oppidum ab equitibus oppugnatum est.
3. Victoria duci a pueris nuntiata est.
4. Galli a copiis Romanis superabuntur.
5. Pauci clamorem captivi audiverunt.
6. Omnes barbari imperatorem Romanum timent.
7. Victoriae multae Romanis nuntiabuntur.
8. Gallorum telis vulneraberis.
9. Onera multa a captivis portabantur.
10. Paucos equites in oppidum duxerat.

XVIII. (Ex. 52–54)

1. Multi cives barbarorum telis vulnerati erunt.
2. Omnia Gallorum oppida vastata erant.
3. Victoria ab equitibus nuntiata erit.
4. Imperatoris consilio servati eramus.
5. Onera ingentia miseri captivi portabant.
6. Puerorum clamoribus urbs servata erat.
7. Pedites oppidum telis oppugnaverunt.
8. Imperator magnas peditum copias in urbem ducet.
9. Omnia pericula ab equitibus vitata erant.
10. Dux bonus clamores hostium non timet.

XIX. (Ex. 55–57)

1. Magnae barbarorum copiae a nostris non timentur.
2. Hostium clamoribus nostri non terrebuntur.
3. Belli periculis non terremini.
4. Urbs a Labieno tenebatur.
5. Pars militum urbem iam occupaverat.
6. Populus Romanus timetur.
7. Hostium partem terruimus, partem superavimus.
8. Imperator milites in castra iam duxerat.
9. Oppidum a nostris tenebitur.
10. Barbari nostrorum telis territi sunt.

XX. (Ex. 58–60)

1. Puer a patre monitus erit.
2. Barbaros terra marique superavimus.
3. Filius paterque in castra maturabant.
4. Belli periculis, fili, non territus eris.
5. Labienus ab imperatore monitus erat.
6. Terra marique Galli superabantur.
7. Urbem pars peditum tenebat.
8. Nostri magna onera portabant.
9. Periculo pedites non territi erant.
10. A Populo Romano non territi erunt.

XXI. (Ex. 61–63)

1. Exercitus Romanus hostium impetum sustinebat.
2. Terra deorum consiliis regitur.
3. Captivi in oppidum ducentur.
4. Cives hostium impetum sustinuerunt.
5. Multae urbes a Romanis reguntur.
6. Exercitus Romani saepe contra barbaros ducebantur.
7. Imperator Romanus multos Gallorum impetus sustinuit.
8. Terra marique contra Romanos ducemini
9. Ab omni exercitu dux amabatur.
10. Filius patris consilio regitur.

XXII. (Ex. 64–66)

1. Imperator pedites dextro cornu instruxit.
2. Exercitus iam instructi erant.
3. Dextrum cornu a Labieno tenebatur.
4. Pars equitum iam instructa est.
5. Multae urbes exercitus Romanos timebant.
6. Labienus ab omni exercitu timebatur.
7. Hostium impetu non terrebimur.
8. Equites in castra reducti erant.
9. Exercitus ab imperatore instructus erit.
10. Pars peditum in urbem ducta erat.

XXIII.   (Ex. 67-69)

1. Civium clamor a rege auditus est.

2. Oppidum aggere munietur.

3. Hostium clamores a nostris audiuntur.

4. A militibus Romanis non audieris.

5. Pueri clamores a patre audiebantur.

6. Urbs multis turribus munietur.

7. Rex equites dextro cornu instruxerat.

8. Militum voces a civibus audiebantur.

9. Multae turres a barbaris aedificatae sunt.

10. Civium miserorum voces a rege non audientur.

XXIV.   (Ex. 70-72)

1. Imperator aciem contra urbem instruxit.

2. Multis rebus exercitus impediebatur.

3. Urbs muro et aggere munita est.

4. Hostium acies contra nostros instructa est.

5. Pueri clamores ab omnibus auditi erant.

6. Multis rebus nostri terrebantur.

7. Urbs magnis muris munita erat.

8. Vox imperatoris ab omnibus audita erit.

9. Belgae Romanorum aciem telis oppugnaverunt.

10. Pars urbis aggere munita erit.

XXV. (Ex. 73–75)

1. Ingentes erant Gallorum copiae.
2. Romani numquam hostes timebunt.
3. Magna fuit sapientia imperatoris.
4. Hostium turres parvae, muri magni fuerunt.
5. Magna erunt belli pericula.
6. Numquam in Gallia exercitus Romanus fuerat.
7. Magnus est numerus captivorum.
8. Omnes in castris eramus.
9. Barbari non semper audaces sunt.
10. Magna fuerit nostrorum victoria.

XXVI. (Ex. 76–78)

1. Altior erat turris quam murus.
2. Galliae flumina latissima sunt.
3. Acerrimo impetu barbaros superabant.
4. Fortiores erant equites quam pedites.
5. Nihil gravius est belli periculo.
6. Civium onera gravissima sunt.
7. Barbari Romanis non fortiores erant.
8. Ducis consilia audacissima fuerunt.
9. Hostium copiae ingentiores quam Romanorum erunt.
10. Altissimo muro urbs munita erat.

XXVII.　(Ex. 79–81)

1. Cottae consilium melius quam imperatoris erat.
2. Res facillima erit equitibus.
3. Gallis scuta utilissima erant.
4. Barbarorum quam Romanorum castra minora erant.
5. Nihil melius est sapientia.
6. Plurimi barbarorum equos non habebant.
7. Minimis rebus maxima saepe consilia impediuntur.
8. Nostri minore virtute pugnabant.
9. Arma in bello utilissima sunt.
10. Pueri res facillimas amant.

XXVIII.　(Ex. 82–84)

1. Urbs nostra ab equitibus servata est.
2. Clamores tui a rege audiebantur.
3. Omnes imperatorem nostrum amamus.
4. Equites in silvis se celabant.
5. Victoriam mihi milites nuntiaverunt.
6. Hostium dux me sagitta vulneravit.
7. Eius pater saepe eum monuerat.
8. Urbem nostram aggere et muro muniemus.
9. Pater meus te impediet.
10. Equitum victoriam vobis nuntiabunt.

XXIX. (Ex. 85–87)

1. Hoc onus gravius quam illud est.
2. Hanc urbem virtute sua servabant.
3. Nihil illa urbe pulchrius est.
4. Te non timebimus, Labiene.
5. Haec onera facile a militibus portabantur.
6. Illud consilium utilissimum fuerit.
7. Haec terra numquam a barbaris regetur.
8. Hos in castra reduxerat imperator.
9. Hoc illi non neglegent.
10. Huius urbis muri altissimi sunt.

XXX. (Ex. 88–90)

1. In eadem urbe et equites et pedites fuerunt.
2. Ab ipso imperatore bellum timebatur.
3. Ipse numquam maiorem exercitum oppugnaverat.
4. Urbs ipsa a militibus neglecta erat.
5. In eodem virtus erat et sapientia.
6. Haec mihi ab eodem nuntiabantur.
7. Idem dux patriam servavit.
8. Ipsum bellum a nostris non timetur.
9. Idem tibi a militibus nuntiabitur.
10. Imperator ipse milites laudavit.

XXXI. (Ex. 91–93)

1. Patria, quam omnes amamus, a barbaris numquam regetur.

2. Equites, quos in silva celavit, superati sunt.

3. Onera, quae milites portabant, gravissima erant.

4. Miles, qui victoriam nuntiavit, laudatus est.

5. Pericula, quae vitavimus, gravissima erant.

6. Ea quae monuisti utilissima fuerunt.

7. Regem vestrum, qui barbaros superavit, amatis.

8. Quod tu times, id nos non terret.

9. Castra, quae oppugnabamus, maiora erant quam nostra.

10. Quae vos neglexistis, ea nos non neglegemus.

XXXII. Ex. (94–96)

1. Urbs, in qua captivi erant, bene munita erat.

2. Galli, quorum virtutem laudavisti, nos superaverunt.

3. Imperator, cuius equus vulneratus est, suos reduxit.

4. Romanorum mores omnes laudabant.

5. Militum animos adventu suo confirmavit.

6. Pedites, quorum tela nos vulnerabant, dextro cornu collocati sunt.

7. Hostes, a quibus superati sumus, agros nostros vastant.

8. Pericula, quibus tu terrebaris, nos non timemus.

9. Belgae, quorum impetum sustinebamus, ab omnibus timebantur.

10. Hominum mores non semper sapientia reguntur.

XXXIII. (Ex. 97-99)

1. Tres legiones in Galliam missae sunt.
2. Quinque cohortes in castris manebant.
3. Quattuor cohortes dextro cornu instruxerat.
4. Adventu legionum cives terrebantur.
5. Una legio Gallorum agros vastaverat.
6. Urbs, quam oppugnabamus, tres turres habebat.
7. Sex cohortes in oppido collocatae sunt.
8. Ex Gallia in Italiam contenderunt.
9. Omnes equites in silvis manserunt.
10. Duas legiones Caesar in Belgas misit.

XXXIV. (Ex. 100-102)

1. Rhodo Romam cum decem navibus navigavit.
2. Athenas omnes legiones contendebant.
3. Nihil Athenis utilius est sapientia.
4. Romae ab omnibus virtus laudatur.
5. Omnes captivi Carthaginem missi sunt.
6. Tres legiones Athenas mittemus.
7. Cives suam ipsi urbem servaverunt.
8. Illi cum quattuor navibus Athenas navigabunt.
9. Romae omnes hostium adventu terrebantur.
10. Gadibus nostri fortiter cum hostibus pugnabant.

XXXV.   (Ex. 103–105)

1. Quinto die urbs ab hostibus oppugnata est.
2. Decima legio a Caesare laudabatur.
3. Hoc anno Romani copias in Galliam miserunt.
4. Tres horas nostri cum barbaris fortiter pugnaverunt.
5. Eodem die rex civibus victoriam nuntiavit.
6. Multos annos Romae fuit pater meus.
7. Carthagine quattuor annos mansimus.
8. Omnes captivi illo die liberati sunt.
9. Nostri sex horas hostium impetum sustinebant.
10. Multas horas gravissima onera portabant.

XXXVI.   (Ex. 106–108)

1. Pugnate fortiter, milites : hostium copias superate.
2. Navigate ad Italiam cum omnibus navibus.
3. Hoc proelium imperatori nuntia.
4. Parate bellum, cives : magnum est periculum.
5. Mone filium tuum : consilium meum neglegit.
6. Instrue decimam legionem contra oppidum.
7. Audi patris vocem : semper te monet.
8. Celate arma : rex in urbe est.
9. Laudate deos, cives : hostes superati sunt.
10. Vos Romae manete : nos in Galliam contendemus.

XXXVII. (Ex. 109–111)

1. Monere a me : vita bellum.
2. Fortissime nostri cum hostibus pugnaverunt.
3. Consilio meo regere : magnus est hostium numerus.
4. Acrius nostri quam Galli pugnabant.
5. Cum decem militibus hostium impetum sustinuit.
6. Hostium copias tertia legio facillime superavit.
7. Laudare ab omnibus : nihil laude gratius est.
8. Haec gens numquam a Romanis superata est.
9. Ama omnes : ab omnibus amare.
10. Res nota fuit paucis militibus.

XXXVIII. (Ex. 112–114)

1. Caesaris consilium utilissimum erit civitati.
2. Nihil gratius erit nobis quam bellum gerere.
3. Utile erit nobis Romae fuisse.
4. Facile est parvum numerum hostium vincere.
5. Pulcherrimum est pro patria pugnare.
6. Malum est omnes laudare.
7. Utile erit urbem muris et aggeribus munivisse.
8. Pulchrum est hostes saepe vicisse.
9. Mos fuit Romanorum numquam pericula vitare.
10. Adventu tuo militum animi confirmati erunt.

XXXIX.   (Ex. 115–117)

1. Bonum est a bonis laudari et amari.

2. Mos fuit semper noster ab hostibus non terreri.

3. Utile est civitati a bono rege regi.

4. Difficile erit a tanto numero civium audiri.

5. Facile est a malis laudari.

6. Obsides, quos miseramus, dux liberavit.

7. Haec res, quae iam paucis nota est, militum animos confirmabit.

8. Turpe erit nobis a paucis peditibus vinci.

9. Magnum est numquam ab hostibus perturbatum esse.

10. Utilissimum fuit militibus cum tanto hoste pugnavisse.

XL.   (Ex. 118–120)

1. Legionem ad urbem contendentem hostes oppugnaverunt.

2. Miseros captivos liberaturus erat.

3. Romanos Carthaginem navigantes vicerunt.

4. Barbaros bellum parantes impedivimus.

5. Puerum victoriam nuntiantem audivisti.

6. Hostes bellum parantes non timebimus.

7. Fortissime pugnans a Gallis necatus est.

8. Milites castra munientes ab hostibus oppugnati sunt.

9. Multos dies Romae mansurus erat.

10. Barbaros bellum gerentes nostri non timebunt.

XLI. (Ex. 121–123)

1. Hostium aciem, equitum adventu perturbatam, superavimus.

2. Homines damnatos necabimus.

3. Urbem muris munitam oppugnavimus.

4. Milites a se laudatos in castra reduxit.

5. Equum telo vulneratum e proelio ducit.

6. Per agros ab hostibus vastatos cucurrerunt.

7. Turrem a militibus visam oppugnaturus erat.

8. Hostes gravissimis oneribus impeditos oppugnavimus.

9. Milites ad bellum missos non iterum videbis.

10. Horum adventu non maxime terrebimur.

XLII. (Ex. 124–126)

1. Hostes oppugnemus, agros vastemus.

2. Milites qui urbem servaverunt laudemus.

3. Cum Galli bellum parent, ipsi bellum paremus.

4. Cum socii sint, exercitum mittemus.

5. Cum fortiter pugnavissent, ab omnibus laudabantur.

6. Cum milites non habeamus, bellum non geremus.

7. Ne magnum hostium numerum timeamus.

8. Omnes patrum nostrorum virtutem laudent.

9. Hostium impetum fortiter sustineamus.

10. Naves maiores aedificemus.

XLIII. (Ex. 127–129)

1. Hostes vincamus qui bellum contra nos gerunt.
2. Ne hos timueritis quos saepe vicistis.
3. Imperatoris nostri verba audiamus.
4. Ne patris consilium neglexeris.
5. Cum frumentum miserint, eorum agros non vastabimus.
6. Cum multas horas pugnaverint, in castra reducentur.
7. Cives, cum barbarorum clamores audirent, timebant.
8. Nostri, cum hostes vicissent, ab imperatore laudabantur.
9. Galli, cum urbem muro munivissent, impetus nostros non timuerunt.
10. Ne vulneratos milites neglegamus.

XLIV. (Ex. 130–132)

1. Ne ab iisdem iam hostibus superemur.
2. Galli, cum Caesaris adventu territi essent, bellum non parabant.
3. Cum urbs non oppugnata esset, cives tuti erant.
4. Cuius adventu cum militum animi confirmati essent, vicimus.
5. Patria nostra civium virtute servetur.
6. Ne belli periculo terreamur.
7. Cum dux eum laudaverit, nos non culpabimus.
8. Milites, cum hostium adventu perturbarentur, reduxit.
9. Cum agri nostri vastarentur, frumentum non habebamus.
10. Ne concilium sociorum convocemus.

XLV. (Ex. 133–135)

1. Auxilium ad socios nostros celeriter mittatur.

2. Cum urbs muris munita sit, periculum non timemus.

3. Imperator, cum iam barbarorum clamores audirentur, suos e castris duxit.

4. Nona legio celerrime ad urbem contendit.

5. Equites dextro cornu instruantur.

6. Ego, cum consilium meum neglectum sit, non iterum vos monebo.

7. Galli, cum flumine impediti essent, a Romanis superabantur.

8. Urbs aggeribus et turribus muniatur.

9. Quinque horas socii nostri hostium impetum sustinebant.

10. Ne imperator civium verbis impediatur.

XLVI. (Ex. 136–138)

1. Milites hortatus, ad urbem contendit.

2. Galli his telis in bello non utuntur.

3. Cives in multis conciliis hortabatur.

4. In hac urbe paucos dies morati sumus.

5. Caesar, milites hortatus, animos ad proelium confirmavit.

6. Cum tres dies in hac terra morati simus, iam in Italiam contendamus.

7. His telis in omnibus bellis utemur.

8. Ne multas horas Romae moremur.

9. Mos erat imperatoris milites ante proelium hortari.

10. In hac terra quinque dies morati multos homines, multas urbes vidimus.

XLVII.   (Ex. 139–141)

1. Urbem alto aggere munitam cepit.
2. Faciamus id quod imperator monet.
3. Impetum in nostros acriter fecerunt.
4. Equites nostri ab hostibus capti sunt.
5. Bellum in nostris agris gerebant.
6. Id quod facitis omnes laudabunt.
7. In Italiam celeriter iter faciamus.
8. Galli in Romanorum aciem impetum fecerunt.
9. Cum ab omnibus culpatus sit, idem non iterum faciet.
10. Oppidum nostra virtute capiemus.

XLVIII.   (Ex. 142–144)

1. Milites imperatoris vocem audire non poterant.
2. Flumine impediti iter facere non poterunt.
3. Vult in castris paucos dies morari.
4. Volumus id, quod mones, facere.
5. Id quod vis omnes facient.
6. Voluimus frumentum ad castra mittere.
7. Cives volent urbem muris munire.
8. Patrum moribus uti volumus.
9. Consilium quod cepisti laudare non possumus.
10. Ei qui in urbe erant periculum vitare non potuerunt.

XLIX. (Ex. 145–147)

1. Noluerunt damnatos necare.
2. Malo pugnare quam in urbe morari.
3. Maluerunt suis telis quam tuis uti.
4. Oppidum altis muris munitum oppugnare nolebant.
5. Malent virtute quam consilio vincere.
6. Obsides, cum necare nollent, liberaverunt.
7. Noli auxilium ad nostros hostes mittere.
8. Cum mallent Romae morari quam bellum gerere ab omnibus culpati sunt.
9. Mavis ab hoc culpari quam ab illo laudari.
10. Nostri perturbatos hostes oppugnare volebant.

L. (Ex. 148–150)

1. Omnia belli pericula ferre volumus.
2. Non potuit mecum [1] ad urbem ire.
3. Volet Athenis Romam celerrime ire.
4. Per agros Gallorum cum magno exercitu ibat.
5. Cum omnia ferre vellet, ab ipso imperatore laudatus est.
6. Constituit cum paucis equitibus iter in agros eorum facere.
7. Poterunt maiora pericula quam haec ferre.
8. Cum bellum gereret, ad urbem ire non potuit.
9. Cum in Italia essem, milites ad bellum euntes vidi.
10. Nihil gravius quam hoc tulimus.

---

[1] The preposition cum is placed *after* Personal and Relative Pronouns, the two being written as one word; thus : **mecum, tecum, secum, nobiscum, vobiscum, quocum, quibuscum.**

LI.   (Ex. 151–153)

1. Caesar dux fortissimus habebatur.
2. Cives iam sapientiores fiunt.
3. Omnibus consilium tutum videbatur.
4. Mihi vir egregius videris.
5. Nihil peius hoc consilio videtur.
6. Maximus imperator paucis annis fies.
7. Tu, cum Gallos viceris, felicissimus haberis.
8. Eo die nihil ab hostibus factum est.
9. Non omnes egregii fieri possumus.
10. Vir fortior quam ipse imperator visus est.

LII.   (Ex. 154–156)

1. Populus Romanus Caesarem consulem creavit.
2. Nos eum virum egregium semper putabimus.
3. Ausus bellum in Gallia gerere multas gentes vicit.
4. Noluerunt cives eum regem nominare.
5. A populo Romano consul creatus est.
6. Cum civitatem virtute sua servaverit, eum damnare non audebunt.
7. Omnibus visus est optimus magistratus.
8. Eos qui patriam liberaverant populus consules creavit.
9. Cum grave sit periculum, omnia audeamus.
10. Noli omnes homines turpissimos putare.

LIII. (Ex. 157-159)

1. Nonne bellum in Gallia multos annos gessit?
2. Potesne oppidum quattuor diebus capere?
3. Num turpe est omnia pro patria audere?
4. Hic rex populi Romani amicus semper habitus est.
5. Nonne grata erit civibus exercitus victoria?
6. Num puer grave onus portare poterit?
7. Nonne hoc flumen latius quam illud est?
8. Quis hoc concilium convocavit?
9. Cur hostium numero perturbamini, milites?
10. A quibus agri nostri vastati sunt?

LIV. (Ex. 160-162)

1. Cotta, vir fortissimus, legiones Romanas contra Belgas duxit.
2. Cum clamores civium auditi essent, opem tulimus.
3. Magna et virtute et opibus regnum occupavit.
4. Pater et mater filium suum hortati sunt.
5. Cotta, populi Romani consul, ad urbem veniet.
6. Caesar et Cotta multa bella gesserunt.
7. Ego et tu hoc consilium capiemus.
8. Caesar, vir sapientissimus, noluit regnum occupare
9. Tu et Labienus facile poteritis hostem superare.
10. Mos erat Romanorum sociis suis opem ferre.

LV. (Ex. 163–165)

1. Galli me multa de suis rebus docuerunt.

2. Cum amicus sit populi Romani, sententiam eum roga-bimus.

3. Cum omnium sapientissimus esset, regis filium docebat.

4. Noli me sententiam rogare.

5. Haec tibi omnium pulcherrima urbs videbitur.

6. Maxima pars civium nolebat bellum gerere.

7. Fac tu quod rogo : melius consilium capere non potes.

8. Suos hortatus contra Britannos duxit.

9. Quis te illud docuit ?

10. Mos erat pueri multa patrem rogare.

LVI. (Ex. 166–168)

1. Et frater eius et soror in urbe morati sunt.

2. Ne regibus serviamus, cives.

3. Erat inter urbem et castra nostra flumen latissimum.

4. Milites semper imperatori parebant.

5. Cum numquam hosti cesserimus, non vobis cedemus.

6. Pare patri : noli nobiscum venire.

7. Erant illi homini frater et soror.

8. Romani regi numquam serviemus.

9. Melius erit necari quam Romanis parere.

10. Multa nos de rebus Romanis frater tuus docuit.

LVII. (Ex. 169-171)

1. Cives miseri fame peribant.
2. Puer libris utitur quos pater ad eum misit.
3. Cum a legionibus victi sint, urbe nostra non potientur.
4. Hostes sine virtute vincere nostri non poterunt.
5. Puer, quem litteras docebam, hoc libro utebatur.
6. Omnes qui nobiscum venerunt fame perierunt.
7. A Gallis victi ad castra redibant.
8. Gallorum regno sine virtute potiri non poteris.
9. Cives, fame victi, hostibus cedere voluerunt.
10. Omnes pueros, qui patribus parent, laudamus.

LVIII. (Ex. 172-174)

1. Hunc tibi librum, quem vides, dabo.
2. Imperator sub alta turre stabat.
3. Cives victos adiuvemus : ne moremur.
4. Haec urbs decimo anno ab hostibus deleta est.
5. Caesaris adventus hostium timorem maxime auxit.
6. Exercitus sub murum urbis ivit.
7. Galli hanc urbem deleverunt.
8. Ne civium timorem his verbis augeamus.
9. Tibi, qui patres nostros iuvisti, omnes parebimus.
10. Hic rex numerum equitum auxit.

LIX. (Ex. 175–177)

1. Milites hortatus Caesar in Italiam discessit.

2. Quid dixit ? Non audivi.

3. Caesar has cohortes cum exercitu coniunxerat.

4. Haec Caesar per exploratores cognoverat.

5. Post sextam horam nostri hostium impetum sustinere non poterant.

6. Obsides quos missuri erant non accepimus.

7. Victoria potiri potest, uti non potest.

8. Ab hostibus victus in castra se recepit.

9. Hic locus a Labieno cum praesidio tenebatur.

10. Caesar castra ex loco movit.

LX. (Ex. 178–180)

1. Caesar castra prope hoc flumen posuit.

2. Victis hostibus parcamus.

3. Nostros ab hoc loco in urbem pepulerunt.

4. Patriam a patribus servatam virtute nostra defendemus.

5. Obsides et captivos in castris reliquerunt.

6. Hoc genere telorum Britanni semper utuntur.

7. Post tres horas castra in hoc loco posuimus.

8. A Gallis pulsi ad castra fugimus.

9. Hoc a militibus ad urbem redeuntibus cognoverunt.

10. Romanos in castra fugientes vidimus.

LXI. (Ex. 181–183)

1. Hic propter sapientiam magistratus creatus est.
2. Cum hoc sciremus, non ausi sumus nos recipere.
3. Ab urbe profecti per sociorum agros iter fecimus.
4. Hostes agmen nostrum insecuti sunt.
5. Melius est pro patria mori quam vinci.
6. Ego dux ero : vos me sequimini.
7. Nolumus sine imperatore proficisci.
8. Non poteris eodem itinere redire.
9. Pater meus et mater Carthagine mortui sunt.
10. Omnia deorum consilio fiunt.

LXII. (Ex. 184–186)

1. Nautae ad naves tribus horis redibunt.
2. His orationibus duorum exercituum duces militum animos confirmaverunt.
3. Arbores et flores in hac terra non vidimus.
4. Hostium multitudinem virtute sua superaverunt.
5. Milites nostri laborem non vitabant.
6. Hostium ordines nostri oppugnabant.
7. Dux militibus quietem dedit.
8. Nauta ad lintrem redire noluit.
9. His sermonibus omnes maxime perturbabantur.
10. Complures militum sub arboribus se celaverant.

LXIII. (Ex. 187-189)

1. Aestate cum exercitu Romam redibo.
2. Bellum in Gallorum finibus multos annos gessimus.
3. Haec gens hieme bellum gerere nolebat.
4. Collis a Labieno cum praesidio tenebatur.
5. Omnes cives legibus parere voluerunt.
6. In his vallibus et arbores et flores vidimus.
7. Cur non milites in monte reliquisti?
8. Caesar ad montem cum exercitu profectus est
9. Castra in colle ponere omnes voluerunt.
10. Aestate quam hieme pugnare malo.

LXIV. (Ex. 190-192)

1. In portu plurimas naves vidimus.
2. Puer manibus uti non potest.
3. Quercus quam domus altior est.
4. Animal pedes habet, manus non habet.
5. Ne calcaribus utamur : equis parcamus.
6. Num quercum, puer, numquam vidisti?
7. Cives imperatori domum, laborum mercedem, dederunt.
8. Omnium arborum quercus maxime laudatur.
9. Naves in portu relictae sunt.
10. Castra prope collem ponere constituit.

VOCABULARIES

SPECIAL VOCABULARIES

Exercises 1-3.

I love, ămo (1).
I hasten, mātūro (1).
I fight, pugno (1).
I work, lăbōro (1).

Exercises 4-9.

I wander, err, erro (1).

Exercises 10-15.

I sail, nāvĭgo (1).

Exercises 16-18.

battle, pugna, -ae, 1. f.
country, native country, patria,
   -ae, 1. f.
victory, victōria, -ae, 1. f.
forces, troops, cōpiae, -ārum, 1. f.
   pl.
Cotta, Cotta, -ae, 1. m.
the Belgians, Belgae, -ārum, 1. m.
   pl.
I announce, report, nuntio (1).
I attack, assail, oppugno (1).

Exercises 19-21.

arrow, săgitta, -ae, 1. f.
wisdom, săpientia, -ae, 1. f.
I wound, vulnĕro (1).
I save, preserve, servo (1).

Exercises 22-24.

horse, ĕquus, -i, 2. m.
Roman, Rōmānus, -i, 2. m.
barbarian, barbărus, -i, 2. m.

Labienus, Lăbiēnus, -i, 2. m.
our men, nostri, -orum, 2. m. pl.
not, nōn.
and, et.
I overcome, defeat, sŭpĕro (1).
I like, ămo (1).

Exercises 25-27.

town, oppĭdum, -i, 2. n.
war, bellum, -i, 2. n.
dart, iăcŭlum, -i, 2. n.
weapon, tēlum, -i, 2. n.
plan, stratagem, advice, device,
   consĭlium, -i, 2. n.
danger, risk, pĕrīcŭlum, -i, 2. n.
camp, castra, -orum, 2, n. pl.
I prepare, păro (1).
I avoid, vīto.

Exercises 28-30.

boy, puer, -i, 2. m.
field, ăger, gen. agri, 2. m.
Gauls, Galli, -ōrum, 2. m. pl.
I lay waste, ravage, vasto (1).
I build, aedĭfĭco (1).

Exercises 31-33.

good, bŏnus, -a, -um.
great, large, magnus, -a, -um.
small, little, parvus, -a, -um.
I advise, warn, mŏneo (2).
I frighten, terrify, terreo (2).
I fear, am afraid, tĭmeo (2).
I have, hăbeo (2).

Exercises 34-36.

beautiful, splendid, pulcher, pulchra, pulchrum.

wretched, unhappy, miser, misĕra, misĕrum

shield, scūtum, -i, 2. n.

prisoner, captive, captīvus, -i, 2. m.

Exercises 37-39.

land, terra, -ae, 1. f.

arms, arma (-orum), 2. n. (pl.).

much, many, multus, -a, -um.

into, in (acc.).

against, contrā (acc.).

I rule, guide, rĕgo, -ĕre, rexi, rectum (3).

I neglect, neglĕgo, -ĕre, neglexi, neglectum (3).

I lead, bring, dūco, -ĕre, duxi, ductum (3).

Exercises 40-42.

general, impĕrātor (gen. impĕrātōris), 3. m.

soldier, mīlĕs (gen. mīlĭtis), 3. m.

leader, guide, dux (gen. dūcis), 3. c.

horseman, ĕquĕs (gen. ĕquĭtis), 3. m.

cavalry, ĕquĭtes (nom. pl.).

Exercises 43-45.

citizen, cīvis (gen. cīvis), 3. c.

shout, cry, clāmor (gen. clāmōris), 3. m.

rampart, agger (gen. aggĕris), 3. m.

enemy, hostis (gen. hostis), 3. c.; pl. hostes, "the enemy."

loud, magnus, -a, -um.

I hear, audio (4).

I fortify, mūnio (4).

Exercises 46-48.

city, urbs (gen. urbis), 3. f.

huge, ingens.

all, every, whole, omnis, -e.

Exercises 49-51.

burden, ŏnus (gen. ŏnĕris), 3. n.

few, paucus, -a, -um.

I carry, porto (1).

by (of living agent), a (abl.) (before vowel or h, ab).

Exercises 52-54.

foot-soldier, pĕdĕs (gen. pĕdĭtis), 3. m.

infantry, pĕdĭtes (nom. pl.).

Exercises 55-57.

people, pŏpŭlus, -i, 2. m.

part, pars (gen. partis), 3. f.

now, already, iam.

I seize, occŭpo (1).

I hold, tĕneo (2).

Exercises 58-60.

sea, măre (gen. măris), 3. n.

and, -que (joined to first word in clause).

by land and sea, terrā mărique.

father, păter (gen. patris), 3. m.

son, fīlius, -i, 2. m.

god, deus, -i, 2. m.

I warn, advise, mŏneo (2).

Exercises 61-63.

army, exercĭtus, -ūs, 4. m.

attack, onset, charge, impĕtus, -ūs, 4. m.

keen, fierce, ācer, ācris, ācre.

often, saepe.

I withstand, sustĭneo (2).

Exercises 64-66.

horn, wing (of an army), cornu, -ūs, *4. n.*

right hand, right, dexter, dextra, dextrum.

left hand, left, sinister, sinistra, sinistrum.

on the right wing, dextro cornu.

opposite to, contra (*acc.*).

I draw up, instruo, -ĕre, instruxi, instructum (*3*).

I lead back, rĕdūco, -ĕre, rĕduxi, rĕductum (*3*).

Exercises 67-69.

tower, turris, -is, *3. f.*

wood, silva, -ae, *1. f.*

king, rex (*gen.* rēgis), *3. m.*

voice, vox (*gen.* vōcis), *3. f.*

I hinder, prevent, impĕdio (*4*).

Exercises 70-72.

thing, affair, matter, res (*gen.* rei), *5. f.*

line, line of battle, ăcies (*gen.* aciēi), *5. f.*

wall, mūrus, -i, *2. m.*

Caesar, Caesar, -is, *3. m.*

everything, omnia.

Exercises 73-75.

number, nŭmĕrus, -i, *2. m.*

fortunate, happy, successful, fēlix.

bold, daring, audax.

never, numquam.

in, in (*abl.*).

always, semper.

I am, sum.

Gaul, Gallia, -ae, *1. f.*

Exercises 76-78.

nothing, nĭhil (*indeclinable*), *n.*

river, flūmen (*gen.* flūminis), *3. n.*

brave, fortis, -e.

heavy, serious, grăvis, -e.

broad, lātus, -a, -um.

deep, high, altus, -a, -um.

than, quam.

fiercely, ācrĭter.

Exercises 79-81.

bravery, valour, courage, virtūs (*gen.* virtūtis), *3. f.*

useful, ūtĭlis, -e.

easy, făcĭlis, -e.

difficult, difficĭlis, -e.

easily, făcĭle.

well, bĕne.

Exercises 82-84.

I, ĕgŏ.

thou, you (*referring to one person*), tu.

he, that, is, ea, id.

himself (*reflexive*), se.

my, meus, -a, -um.

thy, your (*referring to one person*), tuus, -a, -um.

his, her, their (*reflexive*), suus, -a, -um.

his, her (*not reflexive*), ēius.

their (*not reflexive*), eorum, earum, eorum.

our, noster, nostra, nostrum.

your (*referring to more than one person*), vester, vestra, vestrum.

bravely, fortĭter.

I hide, cēlo (*1*).

Exercises 85-87.

this, hic, haec, hoc.

that, ille, illa, illud.

Exercises 88-90.

fear, tĭmor, -is, *3. m.*

self, ipse, ipsa, ipsum.

same, ĭdem, eadem, ĭdem.

both . . . and, et . . . et.

I praise, laudo (*1*).

Exercises 91-93.

the man who, he who, is qui.

who (*relative*), qui, quae, quod.

man (=*human being*), hŏmo (*gen.* hŏmĭnis), 3. *c.*

man (*as opposed to* "*woman*"), vir (*gen.* vĭri), 2. *m.*

ship, nāvis (*gen.* navis), 3. *f.*

Exercises 94-96.

custom, mōs (*gen.* mōris), 3. *m.*

arrival, adventus, -ūs, 4. *m.*

mind, ănĭmus, -i, 2. *m.*

I place, collŏco (*1*).

I strengthen, confirmo (*1*).

I embolden the hearts of the soldiers, militum animos confirmo.

I blame, culpo (*1*).

Exercises 97-99.

to (=*motion to*), ad (*acc.*).

from (=*away from*), a, ab (*abl.*).

from (=*out of*), e, ex (*abl.*).

cohort, cohors (*gen.* cohortis), 3. *f.*

legion, lĕgio (*gen.* lĕgiōnis), 3. *f.*

territories, agri (*plural of* ager).

Italy, Ĭtălia, -ae, 1. *f.*

I march, hasten, contendo, -ĕre, contendi (*3*).

I send, mitto, -ĕre, mīsi, missum (*3*).

I remain, mǎneo, -ēre, mansi, mansum (*2*).

Exercises 100-102.

Rome, Rōma, -ae, 1. *f.*

Athens, Athēnae, -arum, 1. *f. pl.*

Cadiz, Gādes, -ium, 3. *pl. f.*

Carthage, Carthāgo (*gen.* Carthā-gĭnis), 3. *f.*

Rhodes, Rhŏdus, -i, 2. *f.*

with, cum (*abl.*).

again, ĭtĕrum.

I see, vĭdeo, -ēre, vīdi, vīsum (*2*).

Exercises 103-105.

year, annus, -i, 2. *m.*

day, dies (*gen.* diēi), 5. *m.* (*sing. c.*).

hour, hōra, -ae, 1. *f.*

I free, set free, lībĕro (*1*).

Exercises 106-108.

hostage, obsĕs (*gen.* obsĭdis), 3. *c.*

corn, frūmentum, -i, 2. *n.*

state, cīvĭtas (*gen.* cīvĭtātis), 3. *f.*

battle, proelium, -i, 2. *n.*

Exercises 109-111.

nation, race, gens (*gen.* gentis), 3. *f.*

praise, laus (*gen.* laudis), 3. *f.*

pleasant, pleasing, welcome, grātus, -a, -um.

known, nōtus, -a, -um.

on behalf of, for, pro (*abl.*).

Exercises 112-114.

so large, so great, tantus, -a, -um.

bad, evil, mǎlus, -a, -um.

I conquer, vinco, -ĕre, vīci, victum (*3*).

I carry on, wage, gĕro, -ĕre, gessi, gestum (*3*).

I conduct a campaign, bellum gĕro.

Exercises 115-117.

disgraceful, base, turpis, -e.

through, per (*acc.*).

to disturb, throw into confusion, confuse, perturbo (*1*).

Exercises 118-120

I run, curro, -ĕre, cŭcurri, cursum (*3*).

I kill, nĕco (*1*).

Exercises 121-123.

I condemn, damno (1).

Exercises 124-126.

word, verbum, -i, 2. n.
ally, sŏcius, -i, 2. m.
safe, tūtus, -a, -um.
since, cum (subj.).
I call together, summon, convŏco
(1).

Exercises 127-129.

time, tempus (gen. tempŏris), 3. n.
opposite, contra (acc.).

Exercises 130-132.

meeting, concĭlium, -i, 2. n.
I hold a meeting, concĭlium hăbeo.
successfully, fēlīcĭter.

Exercises 133-135.

help, auxĭlium, -i, 2. n.
quickly, cĕlĕrĭter.

Exercises 136-138.

night, nox (gen. noctis).
before, ante (acc.).
I encourage, exhort, hortor (1).
I use, employ, ūtor, ūti, ūsus sum
(3) (abl.).
I delay, stay, mŏror (1).

Exercises 139-141.

journey, march, route, ĭter (gen.
ĭtĭnĕris), 3. n.
on, in (abl.); after "make an
attack" in (acc.).
I take, capture, căpio, -ĕre, cēpi,
captum (3).
I make, do, făcio, -ĕre, fēci, factum
(3).
I make a journey } ĭter făcio.
I march

I adopt a plan, form a plan, consĭlium căpio.

Exercises 142-144.

I can, am able, possum, posse,
pŏtui.
I wish, am willing, vŏlo, velle,
vŏlui.

Exercises 145-147.

I am unwilling, refuse } nōlo, nolle,
I do not wish } nōlui.
I prefer } mālo, malle,
I would rather } mālui.

Exercises 148-150.

I bear, endure, fĕro, ferre, tŭli,
lātum.
I go, eo, īre, ivi or ii, ĭtum.
I determine, decide, constĭtuo, ĕre,
-ui, -ūtum (3).

Exercises 151-153.

wise, săpiens.
remarkable, distinguished, ēgrĕgius, -a, -um.
I am made, become, fīo, fĭĕri, factus
sum.
I consider, hăbeo (2).
I seem, vĭdeor, -ēri, visus sum (2).
brother, frāter (gen, frātris), 3. m.

Exercises 154-156

consul, consul, -is, 3. m.
magistrate, magistrātus, -ūs, 4. m.
I elect, appoint, creo (1).
I name, call, nōmino (1).
I think, pŭto (1).
I dare, audeo, -ēre, ausus sum
(2).

Exercises 157-159.

friend, ămīcus, -i, 2. m.
who (interrogative), quis, quid.
why, cur.

Exercises 160–162.

kingdom, kingship, sovereignty, regnum, -i, 2. n.

protection, garrison, praesĭdium, -i, 2. n.

Verona, Vĕrōna, -ae, 1. f.

mother, māter (gen. mātris).

aid, ŏpem (gen. ŏpis), 3. f. (no nom. sing.).

wealth, ŏpes (pl.), 3. f.

I bear aid, ŏpem fĕro.

I come, vĕnio, -ire, vēni, ventum (4).

I hold, maintain, obtĭneo (2).

I obtain, pŏtior (4) (abl.).

Exercises 163–165.

a Briton, Brĭtannus, -i, 2. m.

opinion, sententia, -ae, 1. f.

letters, littĕrae, -ārum, 1. f. pl.

concerning, about, de (abl.).

I ask, rŏgo (1).

I teach, dŏceo, -ēre, dŏcui, doctum (2).

detain, tĕneo (2).

much (=many things), multa (n. pl.).

Exercises 166–168.

brother, frāter (gen. frātris), 3. m.

sister, sŏror (gen. sŏrōris), 3. f.

among, between, inter (acc.).

I obey, pāreo (2) (dat.).

I am subject to, servio (4) (dat.).

I yield, cēdo, -ēre, cessi, cessum (3).

Exercises 169–171.

hunger, fămes, -is, 3. f.

book, lĭber (gen. libri), 2. m.

without, sĭne (abl.).

I obtain (possession of), pŏtior (4) (abl.).

I perish, pĕreo, -īre, -ii, -ĭtum (compound of eo).

I return, rĕdeo, -īre, -ii, -ĭtum (compound of eo).

Exercises 172–174.

I give, do, dăre, dĕdi, dătum (1).

I help, iŭvo, -āre, iūvi, iūtum (1).

I help, adiŭvo, -āre, adiūvi, adiū- tum (1).

I stand, sto, -āre, stĕti, stătum (1).

I destroy, dēleo, -ēre, dēlēvi, dēlē- tum (2).

I increase, augeo, -ēre, auxi, auc- tum (2).

under, beneath, sub (abl. ordinarily, acc. after " motion to ").

Exercises 175–177.

place, lŏcus, -i, 2. m. (neut. plur. lŏca).

spy, scout, explōrātor, gen. explōr- ātōris, 3. m.

after, post (acc.).

I move, mŏveo, -ēre, mōvi, mōtum (2).

I say, tell, dīco, -ĕre, dixi, dictum (3).

I depart, discēdo, -ĕre, discessi, discessum (3).

I join, coniungo, -ĕre, coniunxi, coniunctum (3).

I ascertain, cognosco, -ĕre, cognōvi, cognĭtum (3).

I receive, accept, accĭpio, -ĕre, accēpi, acceptum (3).

I betake myself, retreat, me rĕ- cĭpio, -ĕre, rĕcēpi, rĕceptum (3).

Exercises 178–180.

near, prŏpe (acc.).

kind, sort, gĕnus (gen. gĕnĕris), 3. n.

I place, pōno, -ĕre, pŏsui, pŏsĭtum (3).

I pitch camp, castra pōno.

I spare, parco, -ĕre, pĕperci, parsum (3) (dat.).

I drive, rout, pello, -ĕre, pĕpŭli, pulsum (3).

I fly, flee, fŭgio, -ĕre, fūgi, fŭgĭtum (3).

I leave, rĕlinquo, -ĕre, rĕlīqui, rĕlictum (3).

I defend, dēfendo, -ĕre, dēfendi, dēfensum (3).

I believe, crēdo, -ĕre, crēdidi, crēdĭtum (3) (dat.).

Exercises 181–183.

line of march, column, agmen (gen. agmĭnis), 3. n.

on account of, propter (acc.).

I know, scio (4).

I set out, start, prŏfīciscor, -i, prŏfectus sum (3).

I follow, sĕquor, -i, sĕcūtus sum (3).

I follow up, I pursue, insĕquor, -i, insĕcūtus sum (3).

I die, mŏrior, -i, mortuus sum (3).

several, complūres, -ium, 3. (pl. adj.).

Exercises 184–186.

sailor, nauta, -ae, 1.

talk, conversation, sermo (gen. sermōnis), 3.

work, lăbor (gen. lăbōris), 3.

tree, arbor (gen. arbŏris), 3.

flower, flōs (gen. flōris), 3.

bone, ŏs (gen. ossis), 3.

mouth, face, ōs (gen. ōris), 3.

boat, linter (gen. lintris), 3.

foot, pēs (gen. pĕdis), 3.

rest, quiēs (gen. quiētis), 3.

multitude, multĭtūdo (gen. multĭtūdĭnis), 3.

rank, ordo (gen. ordĭnis), 3.

speech, ōrātio (gen. ōrātiōnis), 3.

reward, mercēs (gen. mercēdis), 3.

Exercises 187–189.

fleet, classis (gen. classis), 3.

fraud, fraus (gen. fraudis), 3.

summer, aestas (gen. aestātis), 3.

safety, sălūs (gen. sălūtis), 3.

end, fīnis (gen. fīnis), 3.

boundaries, fīnes (gen. fīnium), 3. (pl.)

mountain, mons (gen. montis), 3.

law, lex (gen. lēgis), 3.

winter, hiems (gen. hiĕmis), 3.

disaster, clādes (gen. clādis), 3

valley, vallis (gen. vallis), 3.

hill, collis (gen. collis), 3.

flock, grex (gen. grĕgis), 3.

bridge, pons (gen. pontis), 3

peace, pax (gen. pācis), 3.

I sustain a disaster, clādem accĭpio.

Exercises 190–192.

spur, calcar (gen. calcāris), 3.

harbour, portus, -ūs, 4.

oak, quercus, -ūs, 4.

lightning, fulgur (gen. fulgŭris), 3.

flashes of lightning, pl. of fulgur.

body, corpŭs (gen. corpŏris), 3.

knee, gĕnu, -ūs, 4.

house, dŏmŭs, -ūs, 4.

hand, band, mănus, -us, 4.

animal, ănĭmal (gen. ănĭmālis), 3.

poem, pŏēma (gen. pŏēmătis), 3.

name, nōmen (gen. nōmĭnis), 3.

milk, lac (gen. lactis), 3.

net, rēte (gen. rētis), 3.

head, căput (gen. căpĭtis), 3.

ENGLISH-LATIN

N.B.—The numbers after some of the Latin words refer to the Special
Vocabularies in which further details may be found.

able, I am, possum.
about, de (*abl.*).
accept, I, accĭpio (175).
account of, on, propter (*acc.*).
adopt plan, I, consĭlium căpio (139).
advice, consĭlium.
advise, I, mŏneo.
affair, res.
afraid, I am, tĭmeo.
after, post (*acc.*).
again, ĭtĕrum.
against, contrā (*acc.*).
aid, ŏpem (160).
all, omnis.
ally, sŏcius.
already, iam.
always, semper.
am, I, sum.
among, inter.
and, et.
animal, ănĭmal.
announce, I, nuntio.
appoint, I, creo (154).
arms, arma (37).
army, exercĭtus (61).
arrival, adventus (94).
arrow, săgitta.
ascertain, I, cognosco (175).
ask, I, rŏgo.
assail, I, oppugno.
Athens, Athēnae.

attack, I, oppugno.
attack, an, impĕtus (61).
avoid, I, vīto.

bad, mălus.
band, mănus (190).
barbarian, barbărus.
base, turpis.
battle, pugna, proelium.
bear, I, fĕro (148).
beautiful, pulcher (34).
become, I, fīo (151).
before, ante (*acc.*).
behalf of, on, pro (*abl.*).
Belgians, Belgae.
believe, I, crēdo (178).
beneath, sub (172).
best (*adj.*), optĭmus.
best (*adv.*), optĭmē.
betake myself, I, me rĕcĭpio (175).
better (*adj.*), mĕlior.
better (*adv.*), mĕlius.
between, inter (*acc.*).
blame, I, culpo.
boat, linter (184).
body, corpus (190).
bold, audax.
bone, ŏs (184).
book, lĭber (169).
both . . . and, et . . . et.
boundaries, fīnes (187).

boy, puer (28).
brave, fortis.
bravely, fortĭter.
bravery, virtūs (79).
bridge, pons (187).
bring, I, dūco (37).
Briton, Brĭtannus.
broad, lātus.
brother, frāter (151).
build, I, aedĭfĭco.
burden, ŏnus (49).
by (with persons), a, ab (abl.).

Cadiz, Gādes (110).
Caesar, Caesar (70).
call, I, nōmĭno.
call together, I, convŏco.
camp, castra (25).
campaign, I conduct a, bellum gĕro (112).
can, I, possum.
captive, captīvus.
capture, I, căpio (139).
carry, I, porto.
carry on, I, gĕro (112).
Carthage, Carthāgo (100).
cavalry, ĕquĭtes (40).
charge, a, impĕtus (61).
citizen, cīvis (43).
city, urbs (46).
cohort, cŏhors (97).
column, agmen (181).
come, I, vĕnio (160).
concerning, dē (abl.).
condemn, I, damno.
conduct, I, gĕro (112).
confuse, I, perturbo.
confusion, I throw into, perturbo.
conquer, I, vinco (112).
consider, I, hăbeo.
consul, consul (154).
conversation, sermo (184).

corn, frūmentum.
Cotta, Cotta.
country, native country, patria.
courage, virtūs (79).
cry, clāmor (43).
custom, mōs (94).

danger, pĕrīcŭlum.
dare, I, audeo (154).
daring, audax.
dart, iăcŭlum.
day, dies (103).
decide, I, constĭtuo (148).
deep, altus.
defeat, I, sŭpĕro.
defend, I, dēfendo (178).
delay, I, mŏror (136).
depart, I, discēdo (175).
destroy, I, dēleo (172).
detain, I, tĕneo (163).
determine, I, constĭtuo (148).
device, consĭlium.
difficult, diffĭcĭlis.
die, I, mŏrior (181).
disaster, clādes (187).
disgraceful, turpis.
distinguished, ēgrĕgius.
disturb, I, perturbo.
do, I, făcio (139).
draw, up I, instruo (64).
drive, I, pello (178).

easily, făcĭle.
easy, făcĭlis.
eight, octo.
eighth, octāvus, -a, -um.
elect, I, creo (164).
eleven, undĕcim.
eleventh, undĕcĭmus, -a, -um.
embolden the hearts, I, ănĭmos confirmo.
employ, I, ūtor (136).

encourage, I, hortor (136).
end, fīnis (187).
endure, I, fĕro (148).
enemy, hostis (43).
every, omnis.
everything, omnia.
evil, mălus.
exhort, I, hortor (146).

face, ōs (184).
father, păter (58).
fear, tīmor (88).
fear, I, tĭmeo.
few, paucus.
field, ăger (28).
fierce, ācer (61).
fiercely, ācrĭter.
fifth, quintus.
fight, I, pugno.
first, prīmus.
five, quinque.
flee, I, fŭgio (178).
fleet, classis (187).
flock, grex (187).
flower, flōs (184).
fly, I, fŭgio (178).
follow, I, sĕquor (181).
follow up, I, insĕquor (181).
foot, pēs (184).
foot-soldier, pĕdes (52).
forces, cōpiae.
form a plan, I, consilĭum căpio (139).
fortify, I, mūnio.
fortunate, fēlix.
four, quattuor.
fourth, quartus.
fraud, fraus (187).
free, I set, lībĕro.
friend, ămīcus.
frighten, I, terreo.
from, a, ab (abl.).
from (=out of), e, ex (abl.).

garrison, praesĭdium.
Gaul, Gallia.
Gauls, the, Galli.
general, impĕrātor (40).
give, I, do (172).
go, I, eo.
god, deus (58).
good, bŏnus.
great, magnus.
great, so, tantus.
guide, dux (40).
guide, I, rĕgo.

hand, mănus (190).
happy, fēlix.
harbour, portus (190).
hasten, mātūro, contendo (97).
have, I, hăbeo.
he, is.
head, căput (190).
hear, audio.
hearts, I embolden the, ănĭmo
    confirmo.
heavy, grăvis.
help, auxĭlium.
help, I, iŭvo or adiŭvo (172).
her (see 82).
hide, I, cēlo.
high, altus.
hill, collis.
himself (see 82 and 88).
hinder, I, impĕdio.
his (see 82).
hold, I, tĕneo.
hold kingship, I, regnum obtĭneo.
hold a meeting, I, concĭlium hăbeo.
horn, cornu (64).
horse, ĕquus.
horseman, ĕquĕs (40).
hostage, obsĕs (106).
hour, hōra.
house, dŏmus (190).

huge, ingens.
hunger, fămes (169).

I, ĕgŏ.
in, in (abl.).
increase, I, augeo (172).
infantry, pĕdītes (52).
into, in (acc.).
Italy, Ĭtălia.

join, I, coniungo (175).
journey, ĭter (139).

keen, ācer (61).
kill, I, nĕco.
kind, gĕnus (178).
king, rex (67).
kingdom, kingship, regnum.
knee, gĕnu (190).
know, I, scio.
known, nōtus.

Labienus, Lăbiēnus.
land, terra.
large, magnus.
large, so, tantus.
law, lex (187).
lay waste, I, vasto.
lead, I, dūco (37).•
lead back, I, rĕdūco (64).
leader, dux (40).
leave, I, rĕlinquo (178).
left, left hand, sĭnister (64).
legion, lĕgio (97).
less, mĭnor.
letters, littĕrae.
lightning, fulgur (190).
like, I, ămo.
line, line of battle, ăcies (70).
line of march, agmen (181).
little, parvus.
loud, magnus.
love, I, ămo.

made, I am, fīo (151).
magistrate, măgistrātus (154).
maintain, I, obtĭneo.
make, I, făcio (139).
man, hŏmo or vir (91).
many, multus.
march, ĭter (139).
march, I, contendo (97), ĭter făcio (139).
march, line of, agmen (181).
matter, res (70).
meeting, concĭlium (130).
milk, lac (190).
mind, ănĭmus (94).
most, plūrĭmus.
mother, māter (160).
mountain, mons (187).
mouth, ōs (184).
move, I, mŏveo (175).
much, multus (37).
multitude, multĭtūdo (184).
my, meus.

name, nōmen (190).
name, I, nōmĭno.
nation, gens (109).
near, prŏpe (acc.).
neglect, I, neglĕgo (37).
net, rēte (190).
never, numquam.
night, nox (136).
nine, nŏvem.
ninth, nōnus.
not, nōn.
nothing, nĭhil (76).
now, iam.
number, nŭmĕrus.

oak, quercus (190).
obey, I, pāreo (166).
obtain, I }
obtain possession of, I } pŏtior (169).

often, saepe.
on, in (*abl.*).
one, ūnus.
opinion, sententia.
opposite, contra (*acc.*).
overcome, I, sŭpĕro.

part, pars (55).
peace, pax (187).
people, pŏpŭlus.
perish, pĕreo (169).
pitch camp, I, castra pōno (178).
place, lŏcus.
place, I, collŏco.
plan, consĭlium.
pleasant, grātus.
poem, poēma (190).
praise, laus (109).
praise, I, laudo.
prefer, I, mālo.
prepare, I, păro.
preserve, I, servo.
prevent, I, impĕdio.
prisoner, captīvus.
protection, praesĭdĭum.
pursue, insĕquor.

quickly, celĕriter.

race, gens (109).
rampart, agger (43).
rank, ordo (184).
rather, I would, mālo (145).
ravage, I, vasto.
receive, I, accĭpio (175).
refuse, I, nōlo (145).
remain, I, măneo (97).
remarkable, ēgrĕgius.
report, I, nuntio.
rest, quies (184).
retreat, I, me rĕcĭpio (175).

return, I, rĕdeo (169).
reward, merces (184).
Rhodes, Rhŏdus.
right, right hand, dexter (64)
risk, pĕrĭcŭlum.
river, flūmen (76).
Roman, Rōmānus.
Rome, Rōma.
rout, I, pello.
route, ĭter.
rule, I, rĕgo.
run, I, curro (118).

safe, tūtus.
safety, sălūs (187).
sail, I, nāvĭgo.
sailor, nauta.
same, ĭdem.
save, I, servo.
say, I, dīco (175).
scout, explōrātor (175).
sea, măre (58).
second, sĕcundus.
see, I, vĭdeo (100).
seem, I, vĭdeor (151).
seize, I, occŭpo.
self, ipse.
send, I, mitto (97).
serious, grăvis.
set free, I, lī bĕro.
set out, I, prŏfĭciscor (181).
seven, septem.
seventh, septĭmus.
several, complūres.
shield, scūtum.
ship, nāvis (91).
shout, clāmor (43).
since, cum (*subj.*).
sister, sŏror (166).
six, sex.
sixth, sextus.
small, parvus.

soldier, mīlĕs (40).
son, fīlius.
sort, gĕnus (178).
sovereignty, regnum.
spare, I, parco (178).
speech, ōrātio (184).
splendid, pulcher (34).
spur, calcar (190).
spy, explōrātor (175).
stand, I, sto (172).
start, I, prŏfīciscor (181).
state, cīvĭtas (106).
stay, I, mŏror (136).
stratagem, consĭlium.
strengthen, I, confirmo (94).
subject to, I am, servio.
successful, fēlix.
successfully, fēlīcĭter.
summer, aestas (187).
summon, I, convŏco.
sustain a disaster, I, clādem accĭpio (187).

take, I, căpio (139).
talk, sermo (184).
teach, I, dŏceo (163).
tell, I, dīco (175).
ten, dĕcem.
tenth, dĕcĭmus.
terrify, I, terreo.
territories, agri.
than, quam.
that, is, ea, id, or ille, illa, illud (when—who, qui, quae, quod).
their (see 82).
thing, res (70).
think, I, pŭto.
third, tertius.
this, hic, haec, hoc.
thou, tū.
three, tres.
through, per (acc.).

throw into confusion, I, perturbo.
time, tempus (127).
to (after word of motion), ad (acc.)
together, I call, convŏco.
tower, turris (67).
town, oppĭdum.
tree, arbor (184).
troops, cōpiae.
twelfth, duŏdĕcĭmus.
twelve, duŏdĕcim.
twentieth, vīcēsĭmus.
twenty, vīginti.
two, duo.

under, sub (172).
unhappy, mĭser (34).
unwilling, I am, nōlo.
use, I, ūtor (136).
useful, ūtĭlis.

valley, vallis (187).
valour, virtūs (79).
Verona, Vĕrōna.
victory, victōria.
voice, vox (67).

wage war, I, bellum gĕro (112).
wall, mūrus.
wander, I, erro.
war, bellum.
warn, mŏneo.
waste, I lay, vasto.
wealth, ŏpes (160).
weapon, tēlum.
welcome, grātus.
well, bĕne.
what (rel.), quod.
what (interrog.), quid.
who (rel.), qui.
who (interrog.), quis.
whole, omnis.

why, cur.
willing, I am, vŏlo.
wing (*of army*), cornu (64).
winter, hiems (187),
wisdom, săpientia.
wise, săpiens.
wish, I, vŏlo (142).
wish, I do not, nōlo (145).
with (*with person*), cum (*abl.*).
without, sĭne (*abl.*).
withstand, I, sustĭneo.

wood, silva.
word, verbum.
work, lăbor (184).
work, I, lăbōro.
wound, I, vulnĕro.
wretched, mĭser (34).

year, annus.
yield, I, cēdo (166).
you (*see 82*).
your (*see 82*).

LATIN-ENGLISH

a, ab, by, from.
accĭpio, I receive, sustain.
ācer, keen, fierce.
ăcies, line, line of battle.
ācrĭter, fiercely
ad, to.
adiŭvo, I help.
adventus, arrival.
aedĭfico, I build.
aestas, summer.
ăger, field ; (plural) territories.
agger, rampart.
agmen, column, line of march.
altus, high, deep.
ămĭcus, friend.
ămo, I love, like.
ănĭmal, animal.
ănĭmus, mind, heart.
annus, year.
ante, before.
arbor, tree.
arma, arms.
Athēnae, Athens.
audax, bold, daring.
audeo, I dare.
audio, I hear.
augeo, I increase
auxĭlium, help.

barbărus, barbarian.
Belgae, Belgians.
bellum, war.
běne, well.
bŏnus, good.

Brĭtannus, Briton.

Caesar, Caesar.
calcar, spur.
căpio, I take, capture.
captīvus, prisoner.
căput, head.
Carthāgo, Carthage.
castra, camp.
cēdo, I yield.
cělěrĭter, quickly.
cēlo, I hide.
cīvis, citizen.
cīvĭtās, state.
clādes, disaster.
clāmor, shout.
classis, fleet.
cognosco, I ascertain.
cohors, cohort.
collis, hill.
complūres, several.
concĭlium, meeting.
confirmo, I strengthen.
confirmo animos, I embolden the
   hearts.
coniungo, I join.
consilium, plan, advice, device,
   stratagem.
constĭtuo, I decide, determine.
consul, consul.
contendo, I hasten, march.
contrā, against, opposite.
convŏco, I call together, summon.
cŏpiae, forces.

cornu, horn, wing (of army).
corpus, body.
Cotta, Cotta.
crēdo, I believe.
creo, I elect, appoint.
culpo, I blame.
cum (*prep.*), with.
cum (*conjunction*), since.
cur, why.
curro, I run.

damno, I condemn.
dē, concerning, about.
děcem, ten.
děcǐmus, tenth.
dēfendo, I defend.
dēleo, I destroy.
deus, god.
dexter, right, right hand.
dīco, I say.
dies, day.
diffǐcǐlis, difficult.
discēdo, I depart.
do, I give.
dŏceo, I teach.
dŏmus, house.
dūco, I lead.
duo, two.
duŏděcim, twelve.
duŏděcǐmus, twelfth.
dux, leader, guide.

e, out of, from.
ěgo, I.
ēgrěgius, remarkable, distinguished.
eo, I go.
ěquěs, horseman ; (*plural*) cavalry.
equus, horse.
et, and.
et . . . et, both . . and.
ex, out of, from.
exercǐtus, army.

explōrātor, spy, scout.

facǐle, easily.
facǐlis, easy.
facio, I do, make.
fames, hunger.
fēlix, fortunate, happy, successful.
fěro, I bear, endure.
fīlius, son.
finis, end ; (*plural*) boundaries.
fio, I am made, I become.
flōs, flower.
flūmen, river.
fortis, brave.
fortǐter, bravely.
frāter, brother.
fraus, deceit, fraud.
frūmentum, corn.
fŭgio, I fly, flee.
fulgur, lightning ; (*plural*) lightning flashes.

Gādes, Cadiz.
Gallia, Gaul.
Gallus, a Gaul.
gens, race, nation.
gěnu, knee.
gěnus, kind, sort.
gěro, I wage, carry on.
grātus, pleasant, welcome.
grăvis, heavy, serious.
grex, flock.

hăbeo, I have, hold, consider.
hic, this.
hiems, winter.
hŏmo, man.
hōra, hour.
hortor, I exhort, encourage.
hostis, enemy.

iăcŭlum, dart.
iam, now, already.
īdem, the same.

ille, that, he.
impĕdio, I prevent.
impĕrātor, general.
impĕtus, attack, onset.
in (abl.), in, on.
in (acc.), into.
ingens, huge.
insĕquor, I follow up, pursue.
instruo, I draw up.
inter, between, among.
ipse, self.
is, that, he.
Ĭtălia, Italy.
ĭter, journey, march, route.
ĭtĕrum, again.
iŭvo, I help.

Lăbiēnus, Labienus.
lăbor, work.
lăbŏro, I work.
lac, milk.
lātus, broad.
laudo, I praise.
laus, praise.
lĕgio, legion.
lex, law.
lĭber, book.
lĭbĕro, I set free, I free.
linter, boat.
littĕrae, letters.
lŏcus, place.

măgis, more.
măgistrātus, magistrate.
magnŏpĕre, greatly.
magnus, great, loud.
mālo, I prefer, I would rather.
mălus, bad, evil.
măneo, I remain.
mănus, hand, band.
măre, sea.
mātūro, I hasten.

maxĭmē, very greatly, chiefly.
maxĭmus, greatest.
mĕlior, better.
meus, my.
merces, reward.
mīlĕs, soldier.
mĭnĭmus, smallest.
mĭnĭme, least (adv.).
mĭser, wretched, unhappy.
mitto, I send.
mŏneo, I advise, warn.
mons, mountain.
mŏrior, I die.
mŏror, I delay.
mōs, custom.
mŏveo, I move.
multĭtūdo, multitude, large numbers.
multus, much, many.
mūnio, I fortify.
mūrus, wall.

nauta, sailor.
nāvigo, I sail.
nāvis, ship.
nĕco, I kill.
neglĕgo, I neglect.
nihil, nothing.
nōlo, I am unwilling.
nōmen, name.
nōmĭno, I name.
nōn, not.
nōnus, ninth.
noster, our.
nostri, our men.
nōtus, known.
nŏvem, nine.
nox, night.
nŭmĕrus, number.
numquam, never.
nunc, now.
nuntio, I announce, report.

obsēs, hostage.
obtīneo, I hold, maintain.
occŭpo, I seize.
octāvus, eighth.
octo, eight.
omnia, everything.
omnis, all, every, whole.
ŏnus, burden, load.
ŏpem, help ; (plural) wealth.
oppĭdum, town.
oppugno, I attack.
optĭmus, best (adj.).
optĭmē, best (adv.), very well.
ōrātio, speech.
ordo, rank.
ŏs, bone.
ōs, mouth, face.

parco, I spare.
pāreo, I obey.
păro, I prepare
pars, part.
parvus, small
păter, father.
patria, country, native country.
paucus, few.
pax, peace.
pĕdĕs, footsoldier ; (plural) infantry.
per, through.
pĕreo, I perish.
pĕrīcŭlum, danger.
perturbo, I throw into confusion, confuse.
pes, foot.
plūrĭmus, most, very many.
poēma, poem.
pōno, I place.
pōno castra, I pitch camp.
pons, bridge.
pŏpulus, people, nation.
porto, I carry.

portus, harbour.
possum, I can, am able.
post, after.
pŏtior, I obtain, gain possession of.
praesĭdium, protection, garrison.
prīmus, first.
pro, for, on behalf of.
proelium, battle.
prōfĭciscor, I set out, start.
prŏpe, near.
propter, on account of.
pugna, battle.
pugno, I fight.
pulcher, beautiful, splendid.
pŭto, I think.

quam, than.
quartus, fourth.
quattuor, four.
-que, and.
quercus, oak.
qui, who (relative).
quies, rest.
quinque, five.
quintus, fifth.
quis, who ? (interrogative).

rĕcĭpio me, I betake myself, I retreat.
rĕdeo, I return.
rĕdŭco, I lead back.
regnum, kingship, kingdom.
rĕgo, I rule.
rĕlinquo, I leave.
res, thing.
rēte, net.
rex, king.
Rhŏdus, Rhodes.
rŏgo, I ask.
Rōma, Rome.
Rōmānus, Roman.

saepe, often.
sagitta, arrow.
salus, safety.
sapiens, wise.
sapientia, wisdom.
scio, I know.
scutum, shield.
secundus, second.
sequor, I follow.
semper, always.
sententia, opinion.
septem, seven.
septimus, seventh.
sermo, conversation, talk.
servio, I am subject to.
servo, I save, preserve.
sex, six.
sextus, sixth.
silva, wood.
sine, without.
sinister, left, left hand.
socius, ally.
soror, sister.
sto, I stand.
sub, under, beneath.
sum, I am.
supero, I overcome, defeat.
sustineo, I withstand.
suus, his, her, their.

tantus, so great, so large.
telum, weapon.
tempus, time.
teneo, I hold.
tertius, third.

terra, land.
terreo, I frighten, terrify.
timeo, I fear.
timor, fear.
tres, three.
tu, thou.
turpis, disgraceful.
turris, tower.
tutus, safe.
tuus, thy, your.

urbs, city.
utilis, useful.
utor, I use.
undecim, eleven.
undecimus, eleventh.
unus, one.

vallis, valley.
vasto, I lay waste.
venio, I come.
verbum, word.
Verona, Verona.
vester, your.
vicesimus, twentieth.
victoria, victory.
video, I see.
videor, I seem.
viginti, twenty.
vinco, I conquer.
vir, man.
virtus, courage.
vito, I avoid.
volo, I wish.
vox, voice.
vulnero, I wound.